W/50

This field guide marks Wildsam's 50th book after ten years on the road.

Our thanks to you.

"Yours is a torn and wistful beauty, born
On lonely beaches when the tide is low—
Fog tangled in the marsh grass ... a forlorn
Blue heron wading in the afterglow ...
Dull silver lapping on a wet sand-bar ...
And lost wings circling near a ghost-white star."

—*Doris Caldwell*

WILDSAM PURSUITS

Places are endlessly complex: time, geography, culture and happenings layered with millions of stories. And often, one realizes that a place carries a specific heritage, a definitive pursuit that people build their lives around, a common trade or precious resource that might set the course for generations.

For Big Sur & Highway 1, this pursuit is ocean science and the study of the sea.

Big Sur: its coast and sea attract thoughtful, open-eyed folk. We owe many of them for helping us take our love for this place deeper. Julie Packard, Emerson Brown and Kevin Connor were our guides to Monterey Bay Aquarium, its legacy and future. Mark Ley at Ventana and Juan Martín Palafox at Post Ranch extended welcomes and aid; Mike Scutari at the Henry Miller Memorial Library had the straight insight you'd expect. Kate Woods Novoa and Bree Harlen shared heartfelt wisdom about the care Big Sur needs as a landscape and community. Folks at Flying Fish, Chez Noir and Big Sur Bakery chimed in. There's always a special place on our itinerary [real and imagined] for Nepenthe; hope to see everyone there.

WILDSAM FIELD GUIDES™

Published in the United States by Wildsam Field Guides, Austin, Texas.

ISBN 978-1-4671-9979-7

Illustrations by Bijou Karman

To find more field guides, please visit www.wildsam.com

CONTENTS

Discover the people and places
that tell the story of Big Sur & Highway 1

ESSENTIALS 009

Trusted intel and travel info about iconic places and important topics

ATLAS 017

A guide to the key places along road and coast, curated favorites, cities and towns, and a road trip itinerary

ALMANAC 039

Archival excerpts, timelines, clippings and other historical musings

PURSUIT 065

A field guide to ocean science, with notes on habitats, species and working scientists, on shore and below the waves

INTERVIEWS 079

Concise and meaningful one-way conversations with locals of note

STORIES 099

Personal essays and poems from writers with deep perspective on the landscape and culture of Big Sur and the region

DIRECTORY & INDEX 119

NOTES 124

FOLDOUT MAP 129

WELCOME

IT'S BEEN CALLED the most famous road in America. An exalting, at times nerve-wracking, route that hugs the rubbly edge of the continent. What they say is true and then some. South of Monterey and Carmel-By-The-Sea, Highway 1 is a pilgrimage, an epiphany, a panorama, an achievement. It is a tops-down joyride and an advertisement for awe [and cars]. It is also a path, essentially the only one, into an inscrutable and wondrous spot on our map. Is it a town? A region? An outpost without boundaries? Perhaps best to dispense with labels: it is only Big Sur. *The big country to the south.*

I've been coming to Big Sur for 15 years. First with my wife. Now with our family of five. Each time, we arrive in Monterey and we drive this highway, past Monastery Beach and Point Lobos, past the old general store and the Tickle Pink Inn. We veer off Highway 1 onto a narrow and shady loop called Spindrift Road that leads to a small overlook, so close to the ocean that the wavetops dissolve into air and come to rest on your face. The place is more sound than anything else. It swallows you for as long as you let it, an audible accompaniment to standing beneath the old redwoods farther south.

Each year, we return and follow this path. The highway. The bakery. Pfeiffer Beach. Nepenthe. In that way, our repetition of Big Sur and Highway 1 straddles the permanent and the ephemeral. Which is exactly the thing. Big Sur is a thin place, that wonderful goosebumpy term describing the Indescribable: a veil lifted, light cutting through. It is why mystics and poets, seekers of all sorts, have long ventured to Big Sur.

Ten years and 50 field guides ago, we named "Wildsam" after a man who lived just 30 miles north of Big Sur. Sam Hamilton was the writer John Steinbeck's grandfather, and [continuing the blurred lines] also a character in his novel *East of Eden*. Sam was an Irish immigrant of dogged work ethic, quick cheerfulness, equal parts earthen grit and starry imagination. As the novelist put it: "The children loved it when their father's mind went free."

At Wildsam, our aspirations for you remain the same: To lift the veil, to let your mind go free, to awaken in the big country. —Taylor Bruce

SELECTED CONTENT

010 *Planning*

011 *Geography & Traditions*

012 *Ocean Science & Cultural Institutions*

013 *Scenic Drives & Public Lands*

014 *Film, Music & Books*

015 *Issues & Statistics*

ESSENTIALS

Trusted intel and travel info about iconic culture, geography and entry points to the traditions and landscapes of the Big Sur region

PLANNING

TRANSPORT

BUS

Monterey-Salinas Transit
Line 22, Monterey to Big Sur
mst.org

MOTORCYCLE

EagleRider
Carmel
eaglerider.com

LANDMARKS

BIXBY CREEK BRIDGE

Hwy 1

1930s marvel, photo icon. [Seek parking to the south to ease jams.]

HAWTHORNE GALLERY

Big Sur Village

Rare open-to-public design by key architect Mickey Muennig.

MEDIA

NEWSLETTER

Big Sur Roundup

Since 1955, a cut-and-paste community report, printed on Risograph, mailed monthly.

RADIO

KSQD

Grassroots voices out of Santa Cruz.

PODCAST

A Big Sur Podcast

Magnus Torén of the Henry Miller Library hosts deep talks on place.

CLIMATE

Nestled between the sunny beaches of Southern California and the foggy drama of the north, Big Sur inhabits two worlds. Long tendrils of fog ghost over the morning scene. Warm afternoons burn off the haze to reveal the coastal views of legend. August to October brings warmth [and, unfortunately, wildfires]. Rainy season settles in around December, sometimes bringing snow to the high country. In wet years, spring becomes a wildflower collage on the oceanic overlooks.

CALENDAR

JAN	Big Sur Foragers Festival
FEB	Gray whale migration
MAR	Sea otter pups Santa Cruz Beer March
APR	Big Sur International Marathon
MAY	Carmel Art Festival
JUN	World Oceans Day, Monterey Bay Aquarium
JUL	Esalen summer courses
AUG	Zongo Yachting Cup, Morro Bay
SEP	Monterey Jazz Festival
OCT	Halloween Bal Masque, Nepenthe
NOV	Big Sur Harvest Fair
DEC	Christmas Eve at Big Sur Grange

GEOGRAPHY

Notable terrain formations and where to find them.

SALINAN BLOCK
A wedge of granite squeezed by fault zones gives this coast its roughshod texture. Splintered offshoot of the Sierra Nevada. *Pebble Beach*

TIDE POOLS
Salty bastions of life's diversity spurred Steinbeck to cosmic meditations. Characteristic of the region's rocky shores. *Asilomar State Beach*

NEPHRITE JADE
Rare underwater deposits of precious stone with mystic reputation are protected by strict rules after a history of harvesting. *Jade Cove*

MANGANESE
Deposits of manganese garnet in the hills wash down to turn beach sand a rich wine color. *Pfeiffer Beach*

REDWOOD FOREST
Big Sur holds the southernmost habitat of coast redwood, some centuries old, 10 yards in diameter. *Colonial Tree*

SEAMOUNT
Underwater mountain slopes shelter coral, sponges, rare and still-unknown species. *Davidson Seamount*

TRADITIONS

The region's heritage of creativity, natural wonder and contemplation.

Writing	Big Sur, historically hard to reach in real life, weaves through American writing; Salinas and Monterey shaped Steinbeck. *Henry Miller Memorial Library*
Spirituality	A seekers' landscape, Big Sur holds monastic centers and deep-thought retreat Esalen. *New Camaldoli Hermitage*
Ocean Science	Monterey Bay, much protected, is a globally significant living ecological lab. Divers and ships, manned and unmanned, set out to explore. *CSU Monterey Bay*
Architecture	Epochal views and dramatic, challenging settings inspire a distinct blend of rusticity, daring modernism and eco-sustainability. *Nepenthe*
Mutual Aid	Remote living on rugged lands fosters an ethos of neighbor helping neighbor. *The Big Share, Monday nights*

OCEAN SCIENCE

Key places on a coast known for diverse life, exploration and study.

NATURAL SITES

Piedras Blancas
Teeming rookery for elephant seals
San Simeon

Elkhorn Slough Reserve
Biologically rich tidal marsh
Watsonville

Natural Bridges
Tide pools and monarchs
Santa Cruz

Little Sur River
Nesting plovers, brown pelicans
Big Sur

Weston Beach
Bountiful life at low tide
Carmel

INSTITUTIONS

Monterey Bay Aquarium
Ocean science wonder-world
Monterey

MBARI
The aquarium's research arm offers excellent online seminars

Hopkins Marine Station
Stanford's research outpost
Pacific Grove

Monterey Bay National Marine Sanctuary
San Simeon and Santa Cruz

Seymour Center
Family-friendly immersion
Santa Cruz

CULTURAL INSTITUTIONS

MONTEREY MUSEUM OF ART

559 Pacific St, Monterey

Notably dedicated to California art, including lesser-known treasures like impressionist William Ritschel and abstract painter Joan Savo.

CENTER FOR PHOTOGRAPHIC ART

Sunset Center, Carmel

Traces its origins to the Friends of Photography, a society founded by Ansel Adams, Cole Weston and others. Smart rotating exhibitions.

MISSION SAN ANTONIO DE PADUA

End of Mission Road, Jolon

Still an active parish, one of California's oldest Spanish missions dates to 1771. Eighty-six rustic acres, self-guided tours through a fine museum.

SCENIC DRIVES AND PUBLIC LANDS

Back roads and natural sites across Big Sur.

POINT LOBOS STATE NATURAL RESERVE
More than 1,000 acres of headlands, tide pools and oceanic wonder. Dive the kelp forests, spy harbor seals. *South of Carmel*

OLD COAST ROAD
Four-wheel drive for sure on these 11 miles of dirt through redwoods and old ranches, to a bridge view not everyone gets. *Near Bixby Creek Bridge*

ANDREW MOLERA STATE PARK
Creamery Meadow Trail is the hike/bike to the beach. Ridgeline views, driftwood galore. *Highway 1*

17-MILE DRIVE
A secluded cruise through Pebble Beach, land of glory for golfers and non-golfers alike. When it comes to Monterey cypress trees, Crocker Grove holds the trophy. *Highway 1 to Pacific Grove*

MONASTERY BEACH
Noted for both sandy loveliness and danger, named for the Carmelite spiritual retreat across the road. Rogue waves and undercurrents require caution, but scuba divers plunge in here to reach the edge of undersea Monterey Canyon. *South of Carmel*

SOUTH COAST RIDGE ROAD
Legend among offroaders and overlanders: a rugged twist of dirt to wildflowers, hike spots and vast ocean views. High-clearance vehicle needed. *Via Plaskett Ridge Road*

LIMEKILN STATE PARK
Amid redwood splendor, find steampunky remnants of 1800s limestone milling that helped build San Francisco. *Near Lucia*

GARRAPATA STATE PARK
Four miles of seaside hit a dramatic high note at Soberanes Point, studded with rocky coves, threaded with trails. *Carmel*

CULTURE

FILM/TV

The Sandpiper
Escape to Witch Mountain
One-Eyed Jacks
Star Trek IV: The Voyage Home
East of Eden
Oceans in Glass
The Parent Trap
The Henry Miller Odyssey
Big Little Lies
The Century of Self
Celebration at Big Sur

MUSIC

The Beach Boys
"Big Sur"

Death Cab for Cutie
"Bixby Canyon Bridge"

Frank Sinatra
"It Happened in Monterey"

Joni Mitchell
"Both Sides Now"

Alanis Morisette
"Big Sur"

Kitty Wells
"Carmel by the Sea"

BOOKS

☞ *Cannery Row* by John Steinbeck: The singular Central Coast classic tells a rowdy tale down by the docks of a sardine-fishing town. Today, a garrulous tale of throwback times, but also a lasting human portrait.

☞ *The Stranger* by Lillian Bos Ross: First leg of a trilogy dramatizing a last-wave settler family's century-long epic in remote Big Sur terrain.

☞ *The Hermits of Big Sur* by Paula Huston: Many braids of spirituality knot together on this coast. Huston turns a history of the New Camaldoli monastery into an epic of place, world history and faith's mysteries.

☞ *Big Sur: The Making of a Prized California Landscape* by Shelley Alden Brooks: An environmental historian explores the complex blend of art, politics, economy, nature and engineering that created today's Big Sur.

☞ *Bad Indians: A Tribal Memoir* by Deborah A. Miranda: A collage of insight from a writer of Ohlone Costanoan Esselen descent, delving into the stories of Indigenous people in this region and across California.

☞ *Big Sur* by Jack Kerouac: One for the backpack since Big Jack plumbed this place, his time and his own psyche over ten furious writing days in 1961.

ISSUES

Camping	Big Sur has become increasingly popular in recent years. One side effect: a rise in "dispersed" camping, bringing with it trash, congestion and sanitation issues that bedevil locals. Camping know-how and common respect are needed. A permit process for dispersed camping is in the works. **EXPERT:** *Kate Woods Novoa, website editor,* Big Sur Kate
Logistics	Big Sur's connectivity is spotty; those expecting to take video calls or download big digital files may be frustrated. Meanwhile, there are only a couple gas stations, so it's advisable to fill the tank in Carmel or San Simeon. When parking, remember the needs of emergency vehicles. **EXPERT:** *Rayner Marx, website editor,* Big Sur Visitors Guide
Erosion	Highway 1, that scenic wisp of road, grows more fragile as tides and weather eat at the coastline. A 2021 collapse produced dramatic photos, but also miraculously quick work to reopen the road. The future almost certainly holds more of the same. **EXPERT:** *Lesley Ewing, senior coastal engineer, State of California*
Housing	Among big employers, Ventana has done a notable job of providing employee housing, diversifying Big Sur. As in so many places, recent property booms mean pressure on rents and supply for locals. **EXPERT:** *Martha Diehl, Monterey County Planning Commission*

STATISTICS

343,000........Gallons of sea water in Monterey Bay Aquarium's kelp forest
$16 .... Hourly wage for members of Esalen's extended work/study program
106........................ Length [yards], Pebble Beach 7th hole, pro golf's shortest
45,000 .... Sacks of cement needed to build Bixby Creek Bridge
600 .... Approx. number of tule elk in Los Padres Forest's largest herd
$94,500 .... 2020 auction price for Ansel Adams shot of Point Lobos

SELECTED CONTENT

018 **BESTS**

Food & Drink

Lodging

Experts

Shopping

Arts & Culture

Outdoors

026 **CITIES & TOWNS**

Carmel, Monterey, Salinas, Salinas Valley, Big Sur, Santa Cruz, Morro Bay, Cambria, Castroville, Paso Robles

032 **ROAD TRIP**

A six-day itinerary along Highway 1, with stops for ocean science, golf, beachcombing and deep contemplation

ATLAS

A guide to the lands and places of Big Sur and Highway 1, including curated favorites, communities large and small, and a road trip along the rugged coast

BESTS

FOOD & DRINK

LEGEND

Nepenthe

48510 Hwy 1
Big Sur

A family bastion, landmark, symbol of Big Sur-ness. Ambrosia-sauced burgers. Views that make you use every vocab word.

HOMESTYLE

Deetjen's

48865 Hwy 1
Big Sur

Quiet, candlelit country elegance at dinner. Come morning, a breakfast burrito of trophy proportions.

CALI BREAKFAST

Alta

501 Munras Ave
Monterey

Rice bowls and avo toast in Old Town. Deep local ties.

DESTINATION

The Sur House

48123 Hwy 1
Big Sur

Galaxy-class Ventana ridgeline views. The prix fixe relies on local seas, farms and smart Cali wine picks.

BIG NIGHT OUT

Aubergine

Monte Verde St
& 7th Ave, Carmel

L'Auberge hideaway: a few tables, plush courtyard, serious-ticket tasting menu. Noted for abalone.

RETREAT

Sierra Mar

47900 Hwy 1
Big Sur

Ostera caviar, ranch rib eye, edge-of-continent design drama at Post Ranch.

BREADS

Big Sur Bakery

47540 Hwy 1
Big Sur

Best scones of your life? Pastry patrol arrives early; lunch and dinner are local feasts. Pizza, always.

SUSHI

Treebones Wild Coast Restaurant

71895 Hwy 1
Big Sur

Omakase menu draws a crowd to the yurt resort. Garden herbs, exacting bites. Get your name in.

HANGOUT

Big Sur Taphouse

47520 Hwy 1
Big Sur

The spot to catch a Warriors game and an Underberg shot.

ITALIAN
La Balena
Junipero St btwn 5th & 6th Sts, Carmel
Cozy Tuscan nook: pasta by hand, wine at the forefront, Del Posto on the résumé.

FARM STAND
Earthbound Farm
7250 Carmel Valley Rd, Carmel
Roadside embassy of the time-honored organic brand.

GROCERY
Elroy's Fine Foods
15 Soledad Dr Monterey
Deli and cheese cases like shrines, plus a natural wine trove.

BISTRO
La Bicyclette
Dolores St & 7th Ave, Carmel
Wood-fired oysters and steak au poivre ... well, if you insist.

BRUNCH
Stationæry
San Carlos St btwn 5th & 6th, Carmel
Of all the yogurt bowls in California, this might be it.

CONTINENTAL
Chez Noir
5th Ave btwn Dolores & San Carlos Carmel
Pop-up previews of this new-in-'22 spot stirred excitement for only-here caviar, pintxos, wine picks.

BURRITOS
El Charrito
122 W Market St Salinas
Family-run hero with handmade tortillas and prime taquitos.

ARTICHOKE SOUP
Hog's Breath Inn
San Carlos St Carmel
Serving Castroville's green gold. Used to be Eastwood's place.

APPLE PIE
Big Sur River Inn
46800 Hwy 1 Big Sur
Acclaimed for the throwback recipe.

SUSTAINABLE SEAFOOD
Passionfish
701 Lighthouse Ave Pacific Grove
Pioneer partner to Seafood Watch.

OLD HAUNT
Duarte's Tavern
202 Stage Rd Pescadero
Run by a Portuguese clan since 1894. Big-time garden out back. Crab cioppino on weekends.

NATURAL WINE
Apéro Club
402 Ingalls St Santa Cruz
Sibling to SF's Ruby has tight Cali-maker connections and a hand-built vibe.

DISTILLERY
Venus Spirits
200 High Rd Santa Cruz
Small-batch gins and whiskeys. Beachy spot in Aptos too.

HAPPY HOUR
Alfredo's Cantina
266 Pearl St Monterey
Fireplace, jukebox, nothing fancy, see?

BREWERY
Humble Sea
820 Swift St, Santa Cruz
Wonderfully odd IPAs and saisons.

LODGING

CLIFFSIDE MODERN

Post Ranch Inn

Big Sur

postranchinn.com

Luxe resort on an age-old family homestead. Mickey Muennig climbed trees to craft his eco-mod architecture.

WOODSY RETREAT

Fernwood Resort

Big Sur

fernwoodbigsur.com

Cozy cabins, old-time motel rooms, "adventure tents."

LEGENDARY CAMPOUT

Treebones

Big Sur

treebonesresort.com

Family-run realm of yurts, solar tents and the Twig Hut.

RUSTIC-MODERN

Glen Oaks Big Sur

Big Sur

glenoaksbigsur.com

Fireside rooms and cabins with joyous design. S'mores too!

NATURE RESORT

Ventana

Big Sur

ventanabigsur.com

Forests and ocean blues far as the eye can see. High-living suites, plush rooms and tent cabins. Resident forager.

B&B

Vagabond's House

Carmel

vagabondshouseinn.com

Reno'ed Tudor. A sherry-sipping spot.

TOWN BOUTIQUE

Hotel Carmel

Carmel

thehotelcarmel.com

Crisp, smart design in tune with the art-village vibes.

SOUTH COAST

Lucia Lodge

Lucia

lucialodge.com

Perched over the ocean since 1937. It's way out there.

BEACH LODGE

Asilomar

Pacific Grove

visitasilomar.com

Throwback digs with history: Hearst Castle architect Julia Morgan designed the oldest, hardwood-lined rooms.

HISTORIC INN

Deetjen's

Big Sur

deetjens.com

Wisteria-laced Big Sur icon at a redwood forest's edge.

MANSION HOUSE

La Playa Carmel

Carmel

laplayahotel.com

Ocean and garden rooms, dime drinks at Bud's [time it right].

CLASSIC CABINS

Ripplewood Resort

Big Sur

ripplewoodresort.com

Vintage-feel quarters scattered among riverside redwoods.

EXPERTS

TREES
Lee Klinger
suddenoaklife.org
Arborist and forest health leader. Studies fire's role in oak woodlands.

EMERGENCY RESPONSE
Jeannie Alexander
bigsurfire.org
Medical captain for area's all-volunteer fire brigade, noted for its high level of training.

LAND ADVOCACY
Jeannette Tuitele-Lewis
bigsurlandtrust.org
Leader of the Big Sur Land Trust, orchestrating conservation of private lands.

CONDORS
Joe Burnett
ventanaws.org
Biologist guiding the big bird's wild return. Sanctuary hit by fire in 2020 is being rebuilt.

STEINBECK
Lisa Josephs
steinbeck.org
Archivist at the Steinbeck Center, Salinas base for research into the life and work.

ARCHITECTURE
Douglas Steakley
douglassteakley.com
Carmel photographer's *The Hidden Architecture of Big Sur* gives rare glimpses of knockout homes.

GEOLOGIST
Jonathan Warrick
@jon_warrick
Deploying high-tech [lidar, aerial imagery] to track landslides, river changes, cliffs and bluffs.

MASSAGE
Brita Ostrom
esalen.org
Teaches bodywork, Esalen's own massage techniques and Gestalt awareness.

START-UP FARMS
Kitchen Table Advisors
@kitchentableadvisors
Nonprofit helps kickstart new growers, with many seeds planted in Salinas.

INDIGENOUS CULTURE
Tom Little Bear Nason
@tomlittlebearnason
Esselen Tribe's chair is a source on ecological history and musical traditions.

ARTICHOKES
Pezzini Farms
pezzinifarms.com
Intergenerational growers of heirloom varieties in Castroville, 'Choke Center of the World.

DIVING
Diana Steller
mlml.sjsu.edu
Moss Landing Marine Labs instructor leads kelp-forest plunges.

SHOPPING

BIG SUR ESSENTIALS

The Phoenix

48510 Hwy 1
Big Sur

Nepenthe's shop weaves a boho nirvana of crystals, knit hats, tapestry, jade, pendants, sundials.

PAINTINGS

Big Sur Artworks

447540 Hwy 1
Big Sur

Big color, big landscapes. Local painters pay homage to nature's backdrop.

PROVISIONS

The Cheese Shop

Ocean and Junipero Sts, Carmel

All the fromage and fixings to compose that epic picnic.

FLOWERS

Burst + Bloom

238 Crossroads Blvd
Carmel

Cut flowers, succulents, flowering plants.

GIFTS

COAST

49901 Hwy 1
Big Sur

Local ceramics, art, cashmere shawls, vases. Top-tier soft serve, just for you.

Mother Botanical

47540 Hwy 1
Big Sur

A dreamy stop, French doors flung open under a rosebush sprawl. High-craft handmade goods, tinctures.

ARTS STUDIO

The Shop

1271 10th St
Monterey

Hub for local artists, painting to screen printing.

STATIONERY

The Pleasure of Writing

Ocean Ave at San Carlos St, Carmel

Expert choices for pens, inks, papers.

SUNDRIES

Big Sur Village General Store

46842 Hwy 1
Big Sur

Grab tinned fish, craft beer, wine and gas amid quaint ivy and Spanish tile.

BOOKSTORES

Henry Miller Memorial Library

48603 Hwy 1
Big Sur

More than a bookstore. But also an extraordinary bookstore. A nexus for all things Big Sur.

Pilgrim's Way

Dolores St btwn Fifth & Sixth Sts
Carmel

A community store, a secret garden. Alternative energies since 1969.

Old Capitol Books

Monterey

River House Books

Carmel

ART & CULTURE

WOODWORKING
Johnathan Monte
Big Sur
@johnathanmonte
Surfer-artist making teak chairs in sleek shapes, native-wood cutting boards, cabinetry, furniture.

BOTANICALS
Emmaline Molloy
Big Sur
@valleybotanicals
All-natural essences. Jasmine and calendula body oil, serums powered by herbs.

PAINTER
Lilli-Anne Price
Carmel
lilli-anneprice.com
Plein air oils, rendering the landscape with bold, slightly abstract texture.

GLASSBLOWING
Monterey Glassworks
Sand City
@montereyglassworks
Classes, open houses, artist residencies.

ARTS ORG
Carmel Art Association
Carmel
carmelart.org
Near-century-old collective of painters, sculptors, printmakers. Salvador Dalí was a member.

LEATHER JACKETS
Lance Lindborg
Big Sur
@bigsurkiyote
Full embrace of a vintage motorcycle/retro leathers life.

JADE
David Seefeldt
Lucia, davids
coastalcollections.com
Big hikes and a big cutting wheel make for designs with unearthly glow.

MUSIC ZINE
Lowpass
Salinas
@lowpassmagazine
Passionate coverage of a small-city scene.

POET LAUREATE
Daniel B. Summerhill
Monterey
@bennysummerhill
Poet/performer, author of the recent *Mausoleum of Flowers* and the county's first laureate, 2022.

ARCHITECT
Mary Ann Schicketanz
Carmel
@studio_schicketanz
Sharp-lined modern homes with a naturalist's sensibility.

FURNITURE
Mark Sullivan
Big Sur
Woodworker with legacy built into Post Ranch Inn history.

MUSIC
Kurt Heisig
Monterey
kurtheisigmusic.com
Legendary maker of mouthpieces for jazz stars. Lessons.

OUTDOORS

HOT SPRINGS

Sykes

Ventana Wilderness

ventanawild.org

Famed and popular. Pine Ridge Trail, long closed due to fire, reopened 2021 and needs respectful use. Check the regs!

HIKING TRAIL

Tanbark Trail

Julia Pfeiffer Burns State Park

Five-plus-miler through canyon redwoods. Surreal tin house dates to 1940s.

ROCKY COVE

Partington Cove

Julia Pfeiffer Burns State Park

Old-timey redwood-walled tunnel to an ocean nook.

ANCIENT TREES

Mitteldorf Preserve

Southeast of Carmel

bigsurlandtrust.org

Dewing Redwood: 12 centuries old.

WILDFLOWERS

Fort Ord National Monument

Marina

blm.gov

Baby blue eyes, lupine, rare goldfields.

FISHING CHARTER

J & M Sport Fishing

Monterey

jmsportfishing.com

Rockfish and lingcod are the main pursuit, but this Fisherman's Wharf outfit chases salmon and crab too.

BIKE SHOP

Work Horse

Monterey

workhorsebicycles.com

Top road, gravel and MTB brands, plus solid rental deals.

SURF SPOT

Sand Dollar Beach

Los Padres National Forest, fs.usda.gov

Stunning crescent of sand, popular with longboarders, novices, most everyone.

CLIMBING AREA

Granite Creek

Near Granite Canyon Bridge, Hwy 1

Bouldering. Take on The Young King and The Corridor, but mind the tides.

MOUNTAIN SUMMIT

Mount Manuel

Pfeiffer Big Sur State Park

High and dry route to a 3,000-foot-plus view of the hills and coast.

MUSHROOM OUTING

Big Sur Guides

bigsurguides.com

Wet-season foraging for edible fungi and medicinal flora, with a venerable outfit.

KAYAK LAUNCH

Mill Creek

South of Lucia, Hwy 1

Great place to put in. Paddle south to explore sea stacks, coves and majestic Plaskett Rock.

SAILING

Elkhorn Yacht Club

Moss Landing

elkhornyachtclub.org

Old school, dating to 1946, with two informal bay outings most weeks and a busy racing schedule.

KIDS

Dennis the Menace Park

Monterey

Hank Ketcham, *Dennis* creator, was a local. A wonderland of modern slides and climbing forts.

SCUBA

Aquarius Dive Shop

Monterey

aquariusdivers.com

Home base for a highly active dive club, plunging several times a week. Classes, rentals, guided sanctuary tours.

CYCLING FESTIVAL

Sea Otter Classic

Monterey

April

Rendezvous for many bike-y breeds, with multiple races, tours. Gran Fondo Pacifico loops 50 coastal miles.

FUN RUN

Big Sur International Marathon 5K

April

The lite version of the iconic "run on the ragged edge of the Western world."

GOLF

Pacific Grove Golf Links

Monterey

playpacificgrove.com

The dollar-smart pick in golf paradise, hugging the ocean, British-style.

Bayonet

Seaside

bayonetblackhorse.com

Narrow and pocked with bunkers: just plain mean, one of Cali's toughest.

RACQUET SPORTS

Carmel Valley Ranch

carmelvalleyranch.com

Eight-court tennis and pickleball resort.

SURF FISHING

Salinas River

Castroville

fws.gov

Cast for surfperch and striped bass.

PARAGLIDING

Prewitt Ridge

ushpa.org

Dedicated fliers spearheaded recent road improvements to a longstanding takeoff spot.

URBAN HIKES

Mission Trail Nature Preserve

Carmel

Three chill miles through native woodlands and gardens.

SWIMMING POOL

Salinas Aquatic Center

centralcoastymca.org

Epic glassed-in plunge for morning laps or family swims.

BEACH RIDES

Monterey Bay Equestrian Center

montereybay equestrian.com

Outings amid Salinas River dunes.

BEACHCOMBING

Point Sierra Nevada

San Simeon

Driftwood central, tide pools, all a bit out of the way.

CITIES & TOWNS

Whether surrounded by remote ruggedness, rich farm country or seaside splendor, these communities are noted for their warmth and verve.

CARMEL

Carmel-by-the-Sea was planned and created by artists, which comes through in its visually charming atmosphere, with cypress-lined blocks holding fairy-tale cottages. The square-mile blocks of downtown feel more like a quaint stop in the Swiss Alps than a stereotypical California beach town. [If you're feeling inspired by the local visionaries, pick up a canvas and some watercolors at **IMAGINE ART SUPPLIES** in Pacific Grove first and memorialize the moment en plein air.] Of course, the creative life has its eccentricities, and so does Carmel: There are no street lights [making for pitch-black, starry nights], no national chain restaurants, and no street addresses. Instead, homes are known by names like "Almost Heaven" and "Sea Urchin," whimsy straight out of an English village. Once you've got your bearings, start your day with a tour of Carmel's galleries: **ZANTMAN ART GALLERIES**, Dawson Cole Fine Art, Gallery Sur, and Marjorie Evans Gallery are all standouts, but let your eye guide you among the many possibilities. Next, stroll past the cottages around **OCEAN AVENUE**: **COTTAGE OF SWEETS** for chocolate and candies, The Cheese Shop for your dairy needs, **THINKER TOYS** for puzzles and games. From here, head toward a nook that meets your sensibility: a scone and Earl Grey for afternoon tea at Tuck Box, or a whiskey at the local haunt **SADE'S COCKTAILS**. The most irrestible branding behind the bar around here? Hit the Alvarado Street Brewery's Carmel Bistro and ask about "Yeast of Eden," its series of saisons and wild ales channeling local fruit and mad-science brewing techniques. **FLYING FISH GRILL** takes a cozy, Asian-inflected approach to wild-caught fish, where the almond-crusted Chilean sea bass is the hit on maximum rotation. Seventh & Dolores gives that bodacious six-on-the-shell-and-a-massive-steak energy a modern vibe, with a Niman Ranch partnership and floods of coastal light. Whatever your chosen path, don't miss sunset, whether at **CARMEL RIVER STATE BEACH**, where the river flows into the ocean, or from the patio at Mission Ranch.

OYSTER STOP

Flaherty's

West Coast half-shell goodness for 40 years

POPULATION: 3,220

COFFEE: Cafe Luna

BEST DAY OF THE YEAR: Carmel Art Walk [second Saturday of the month]

MONTEREY

Monterey has always had a knack for reinvention. From its days as the Alta California provincial capital for both Spain and Mexico to its 20th-century heyday as a sardine-fishing port, the city has thrived as far more than a sleepy region's coastal hub. In the 1940s, canneries harvested over 250,000 tons of sardines every season. But after overfishing caused the catch to virtually disappear in the 1950s, Monterey shifted toward tourism, renaming its waterfront business street [formerly Ocean View Avenue] Cannery Row in homage to John Steinbeck's shaggy novel of Depression-era shenanigans. Today, no visit to Monterey is complete without a few hours at MONTEREY BAY AQUARIUM. The city has a thriving marine community outside of captivity too. After the aquarium, stroll along CANNERY ROW, where the factories have given way to saltwater taffy shops and fried-fish stands overlooking the water. [Steinbeck fans, keep an eye out for tucked-away murals.] Wander the final mile along the Monterey Bay Coastal Trail [or pick up a bike rental at BIG SUR ADVENTURES],which winds along the waterfront, frolicking grounds for otters and sea lions. It's not uncommon to catch sightings of whales and dolphins too. Once you reach the trail's end in Pacific Grove, stop by the MONTEREY BUTTERFLY SANCTUARY where, from October to March, thousands of migrating monarch butterflies pass through. After all that animal-spotting, grab a picnic table at LUCY'S ON LIGHTHOUSE and sit back to watch the human parade with a local beer and a wide selection of loaded hot dogs and sausages. The FISHWIFE in Pacific Grove puts a New World spin on the surrounding ocean bounty, its menu hitting Caribbean and Mayan notes. A crossroads of the town's deep roots and fresh energy can be found at the COOPER MOLERA ADOBE, a Boston sea captain's home dating to the 1820s which now anchors a modern culinary corner: CELLA, an Italian-inflected restaurant deeply at home in these Mediterranean-esque climes, and Alta Bakery, which gets the good word up and down this coast. At the far end of the day, PEARL HOUR takes its name from Steinbeck [excellent taste] and cocktail inspiration from fruit, herbs and astrological signs.

BREAKFAST STOP

Old Monterey Cafe
Pancake and waffle fantasia

POPULATION: 29,874

COFFEE: Plumes Coffee & Tea

BEST DAY OF THE YEAR: Monterey Jazz Festival, September

SALINAS

As any Steinbeck fan knows, the author's hometown shaped him, and vice versa. Today's predominantly Latino city has evolved much, but echoes of the great writer still resound here. Start out at **FIRST AWAKENINGS**, breakfast in a brick building erected by a local magnate in 1900. Then dive in at the **NATIONAL STEINBECK CENTER**, which features exhibits about the author's books alongside artifacts. Known as "The Salad Bowl of the World," the Salinas Valley nurtures awe-inspiring produce; head to **THE FARM** to get your fill of seasonal veggies and olallieberry pie. **EL CHARRITO MARKET** follows up with real-deal California Mexican. Oldtown is your local-lore immersion, from murals commissioned to commemorate local life to storytelling locals at classic dives like The King's Den.

LIVE VENUE	POPULATION: 162,791
Fox Theater	COFFEE: The Beerded Bean
Gussied-up, 90 years old, superb neon	BEST DAY OF THE YEAR: California Rodeo Salinas, July

SALINAS VALLEY

In the 1790s, Spanish colonists planted the first grapevines in what is now the Santa Lucia Highlands wine-growing area. Here, you'll find River Road: 33 miles and 13 tasting rooms from Salinas to Greenfield, some as high as 1,200 feet above sea level. Hot mornings, cool foggy nights and high elevation combine to produce much-praised chardonnays and pinot noirs. Syrahs flourish in the slightly warmer, more wind-protected canyons and slopes. Imbibe the full range of valley offerings at **SCHEID VINEYARDS** in Greenfield and Wrath Wines, **MANZONI CELLARS** and Hahn Estates/Smith & Hook Winery in Soledad. **INN AT THE PINNACLES** is a base camp for Pinnacles National Park, a homey, rustic place to stay within easy reach of both plush wine country and the park's volcanic crags.

BONUS WINE	POPULATION: 24,778 [Soledad]
Chalone Vineyards	COFFEE: Viva Espresso Organics
Monterey County's oldest producing vineyard	BEST DAY OF THE YEAR: Salinas Valley Food and Wine Festival, August

BIG SUR

When your jaw drops at the sight of the sea crashing against wildflower-strewn cliffs, inhale: You're here. Once you've absorbed the otherworldly view, explore the deeply layered village that shares the region's name. Start with brunch at **DEETJEN'S**, a regular pilgrimage for both locals and return visitors. Then head out to a local beach to dip your toes in the Pacific on the tucked-away rocks of **PARTINGTON COVE**. Nepenthe commands the best ocean view and also offers French fries and local wine. **FERNWOOD RESORT** is one of several woodsy, casual spots lining the Big Sur River—good for a siesta after a push up one of many trailheads into the hills. **BIG SUR BAKERY** somehow offers the best scones by day and sophisticated dinner by night [primo tote bags, ceramics and jam, all times], and **BIG SUR TAPHOUSE** is the local rendezvous.

SUNDIAL STOP

Phoenix Shop
All your Big-Sur-vibe needs, served

POPULATION: 1,474

COFFEE: Big Sur Bakery

BEST DAY OF THE YEAR:
Winter solstice sunset through Pfeiffer Beach's Keyhole Arch

SANTA CRUZ

After Big Sur's pensive grandeur, Santa Cruz offers a different Cali ethos—more far-out. Just as UC-Santa Cruz cheers on the mighty banana slug as its mascot, natural crunch and good fun imbue the town, from the Sky Glider gondola at **SANTA CRUZ BEACH BOARDWALK** to an only-in-SC crystal consciousness palace, World Of Stones and Mystics. Pacific Avenue is the town's heart chakra, home to **BOOKSHOP SANTA CRUZ** and drag night at The Blue Lagoon. A few blocks away, **BABBLING BROOK INN** offers woodsy tranquility amid the bustle. **CAFÉ GRATITUDE** defines hippie vegetarian food [in a good way]. After enjoying fine people watching in town, marvel at tinier residents in the tide pools at **NATURAL BRIDGES STATE MARINE RESERVE**.

SWEET SPOT

Marianne's Ice Cream
Ask for the 1020

POPULATION: 61,950

COFFEE: 11th Hour

BEST DAY OF THE YEAR:
King tides, December

MORRO BAY

POP. **10,757**

COFFEE **TOP DOG**

Morro Bay finds its namesake in a 23-million-year-old volcanic hunk, "the Gibraltar of the Pacific." **MORRO STRAND STATE BEACH** rambles right out to the dramatic slab of rock. **TOGNAZZINI'S DOCKSIDE**, round the bayside, takes huge pride in serving the catch from waters around here. The **MORRO BAY MARITIME MUSEUM** maintains a small but intriguing historic fleet. Sundowners? Meet at the Libertine.

CAMBRIA

POP. **5,678**

COFFEE **CAMBRIA COFFEE**

Cambria, south of San Simeon, is definitely a town: a stroll through the **EAST VILLAGE** rewinds to the late 1800s by way of urbane vintage architecture. But this place is truly about its forest, one of California's last-standing examples of Monterey pinewoods. **FISCALINI RANCH PRESERVE** sits at the heart of town, laced with trails through vital habitat. **CAMBRIA BEACH LODGE** bunks down on the oceanic side.

CASTROVILLE

POP. **7,515**

COFFEE **LA FORTUNA BAKERY**

"The Artichoke Center of the World"—you have to love it. Pay homage at the **GIANT ARTICHOKE**, which is indeed marked by a huge thistly globe. [Try the hearts, deep fried.] **BIRRIERIA COALCOMAN** is a meaty affair among the Latin American restaurants stacked in the tiny grid. It might all feel far from Fisherman's Wharf, but **MONTEREY BAY COASTAL RECREATION TRAIL** links to the seaside, just 18 miles away.

PASO ROBLES

POP. **31,490**

COFFEE **SPEARHEAD**

Vineyards and wineries ring this wine country crossroads. **GIORNATA** puts an Italian sway on classic reds and whites, orange wines and aperitivi. Across a psychic border, **TABLAS CREEK** is noted as a pioneer of Rhone wines in California and biodymanic farming. At **FIELD RECORDINGS**, Andrew Jones pulls from vineyards hither and yon to create wines as free-wheeling as California itself.

ROAD TRIP

Take a journey deep into the landscape [and spirit] of Big Sur, with a mythic drive, sea creatures, legendary sport and a place for profound contemplation.

DAY 1

THE BIG DRIVE

Threading the Highway 1 needle southward opens up some of the world's most legendary motoring sights.

For any visitor to Big Sur, the odyssey-like coastal drive on Highway 1 provides the high-resolution moments. Revel in the drive, with an eye on the odometer and key landmarks. Start off at **COAST BIG SUR**, a cafe and gallery south of the town of Big Sur. Built in a former redwood water tank, COAST is a modern hunter-gatherer dream of picnic fare and cortados. Pick up a few sandwiches and salads for later—and, just an idea, a soft-serve swirl for now.

After 25 miles [near mile marker 16], stop at the pullout to walk down to a tucked-away cove, a place to enjoy that picnic alone with the crashing Pacific. During springtime, riotous purple and orange wildflower blooms take over the fields across the highway.

After 10 miles, stop for a stroll into **NATHANIEL OWINGS MEMORIAL REDWOOD GROVE**, one of the last and most impressive stands of the region's redwoods, *Sequoia sempervirens,* at the southern edge of its range. It's impossible to come away from a visit with these trees, so ancient, described by Steinbeck as "ambassadors from another time," without a sense of awe.

After 3 more miles, **SALMON CREEK TRAILHEAD** leads to the 0.3-mile hike to Salmon Creek Falls, a 120-foot cascade surrounded by shady sycamore trees.

Nineteen miles later, arrive at **HEARST CASTLE**. Commissioned by the famed newspaper baron and designed by legendary California architect Julia Morgan, the 165-room mansion took more than 28 years to build. Spend a few hours taking an official tour or wandering on your own, exploring the grand rooms, the ornate pools and the grounds—and don't miss the herd of zebras, descendants of William Randolph Hearst's private zoo.

Before heading back up toward Big Sur, one more road trip stop: for more baronial feelings, **HEARST WINERY**, where the tasting menu goes well with tri-tip from the on-site food truck. For a return to the common people, drive 10 miles south to **MOZZI'S SALOON** in Cambria, a cowboy bar built in 1866. The original prospectors may be gone, but tall tales still get told around the two pool tables.

DAY 2

PEBBLE BEACH

Whatever your bag, one of the most majestic American golf courses has the goods.

MORNING Play hallowed Pebble Beach Golf Links, where Palmer, Nicklaus and Woods all had epic moments. A round at PB is spendy [from $695 in 2022] but it's there for you: a public course, arguably the grandest. Pro tip on the famously beautiful, difficult 18th hole: "Aggressive drives attempting to reach this par-5 in two need to send their tee shots left of the tree in the fairway. Or you can safely play to the right of the tree, lay up and wedge onto the green."

NOON From A to B, 17-Mile Drive is 20 minutes, but you're sure to stop. Or keep the camera stashed and simply behold: the Lone Cypress, a Monterey cyprus standing sentinel on a granite headland; the silver-screen-ready coastal cliffs of Point Joe; Crocker Grove, home to venerable trees. Lunch is at The Bench, overlooking the 18th hole.

NIGHT Hang with us here. Tom Watson, five-time British Open champion, once remarked: "Spanish Bay is so much like Scotland, you can almost hear the bagpipes." Every evening since its 1987 opening, a bagpiper has played The Inn and Links at Spanish Bay, closing down the course. Get a sundown drink at Sticks and feel the Highland call.

DAY 3

MONTEREY BAY AQUARIUM

Cannery Row's pop-science shrine conjures a mental voyage by replicating oceanic habitats. Four key attractions:

THE GREAT TIDEPOOL

MBA's most "natural" exhibit nestles in Monterey Bay: spy on cavorting otters and, sometimes, wayfaring whales. Here begins a visitor path from ocean's edge to fathoms deep.

THE KELP FOREST

The first-ever built simulation of this vital offshore biosphere creates mesmerizing, stained-glass-like light effects. Anchovies swarm and swirl within, flashing like a disco ball.

THE NEAR-SHORE HABITAT

Sharks, sea bass, rockfish—all denizens of the Central Coast waters—swim near Cooking for Solutions, a diner-style display on MBA's Seafood Watch and sustainable fish consumption.

INTO THE DEEP

After open-ocean exhibits, a dive-like descent demonstrates underwater exploration and strange wonders: chain-like siphonophores, red bloodybelly comb jellies, giant spider crabs.

MBA's Kevin Connor notes that Wave Crash, a glass tunnel hit by a deluge every 30 seconds, is the Instagram fave here, but has scientific purpose: "It simulates the stressful environment of the tidal zone."

DAY 4

PFEIFFER BEACH

Katie Rose, marine biologist at Ventana Big Sur, shares her notes on a place of rare, wild beauty.

"You take a steep turn off Highway 1, and drop down into Sycamore Canyon. Walk two minutes through a cypress grove, where a little stream meanders along the side. By the stream, there's sand with a psychedelic purple snakeskin-like pattern. Stones of all colors. Beyond the purple comes the finest, whitest, softest sand. At the beach access, you see huge rocks protruding from the ocean. One is a keyhole rock with waves crashing through, perfect to watch the sunset through. In terms of marine life—oh my goodness, it has everything: whales, sea otters, dolphins and white sharks. Every time I'm there, I can picture the Esselen Tribe harvesting mussels or fishing off the beach. You can look at something really close up and small but the real mystery comes from surrendering to the grand hugeness of it all."

DAY 5

THE SOUTH COAST

Even in a Big Sur context, this is remote and wild terrain—with plenty of detours to explore.

What Big Sur locals call the "South Coast" unofficially starts about 16 miles south of Big Sur itself. The region makes points north feel like a hyperconnected metropolis. The area has no electricity grid or water system, but the distance from much of modernity adds to its charm. As well as hardy residents, South Coast is home to much of Big Sur's federal and state land, which means it offers many of the most stunning views to be had by any and all.

South of LUCIA LODGE—site of one of the first homesteads in Big Sur and a beloved restaurant that burned down in 2019—a key sign appears, proclaiming the "Holy Granola" of the NEW CAMALDOLI HERMITAGE, tucked away on a peak above Highway 1. Stop into the bookstore, where a friendly Carmelite monk will tell you about the active monastery and point you toward their homemade brandy-dipped date-nut cakes. During a reverent moment in the chapel, light filters in through an octagonal wooden roof, the bright blue of the Pacific churning through the courtyard window. A gentle hour-long walk along the hermitage's Fence Loop Trail, offers a pick of contemplative benches that look out toward where the ocean meets the sky.

Drive 20 more minutes along the coast to the WHALE WATCHER'S CAFE for a plate of fish and chips and a table on the patio. In summer, blue and humpback whales patrol the waters beyond.

Grab any snacks from the gas station [and use the restroom; they're few and far between on the South Coast] before you head to SAND DOLLAR BEACH. Spend the afternoon enjoying the gentle surf and exploring the largest unbroken stretch of sand in Big Sur—and likely spotting a few sand dollars yourself.

Jeff Norman, a longtime Big Sur historian who died in 2007, left detailed journals of coast life, found now at xasauantoday.com.

DAY
6

ESALEN

Complete your Big Sur journey at a globally famed nexus of deep thought and "human potential."

Aldous Huxley, Ken Kesey, Alan Watts—for 60 years, the **ESALEN INSTITUTE** has been the epicenter of the New Age movement. Founded by two Stanford grads in 1962 to bring together a community of seekers in exploration of human consciousness, the not-for-profit has welcomed tens of thousands in pursuit of inner transformation. The grounds themselves—120 acres perched between mountains and the ocean, with natural hot springs along the cliff—provide an ideal setting for Esalen's workshops, which range from psychedelics as medicine to developing a relationship with death to the sacred feminine to yoga. Book an all-inclusive stay for a workshop [most are three-to-four days], with prices and accommodations ranging from sleeping bag space to suites. If you're looking to stop in for a visit, you can buy a one-day visitor pass Tuesdays through Fridays, which includes a 75-minute massage and access to the hot springs. Spaces are very limited; drop a line via email to inquire. In the past, Esalen has offered public night bathing to visitors; as of 2022, that's not available due to coronavirus-related restrictions, so check back before your visit.

SELECTED CONTENT

040 *Writers of Note*

041 *Esselen Tribe*

042 *Wreck of the* Los Angeles

043 *Hermit Encounter*

044 *John Steinbeck*

046 *Monterey International Pop Festival*

047 *Lillian Bos Ross*

048 *Robert Louis Stevenson*

049 *Jack Kerouac*

050 *Sardines*

051 *Esalen*

054 *Pebble Beach*

055 *Henry Miller*

057 *Houses of Note*

059 *The Keeling Curve*

061 *Nora May French*

062 *Big Sur Folk Festival*

MORE THAN 30 ENTRIES ☞

ALMANAC

A deep dive into the cultural heritage of Big Sur and Highway 1 through news clippings, timelines, writings and other historical hearsay

WRITERS OF NOTE

LILLIAN BOS ROSS Published *The Stranger: A Novel of the Big Sur*, classic settlement tale, while working as an aircraft lookout during WWII.

LAWRENCE FERLINGHETTI Founder of San Francisco's City Lights, Beat publisher, poet. His Bixby Canyon cabin was Kerouac's 1961 refuge.

JACK KEROUAC *Big Sur*, hammered out in a 10-day frenzy, mixes booze and crisis, softened by nature's beauty. Goes to dark places.

DEBORAH MIRANDA Current Indigenous poet. "My father opens a map of California— / traces mountain ranges, rivers, county borders / like family bloodlines."

RICHARD BRAUTIGAN Freewheeling but tortured '60s novelist based *A Confederate General from Big Sur* on local eccentic Price Dunn.

LAURA DAVIS With Santa Cruz poet Ellen Bass, co-author of abuse recovery book *The Courage to Heal.* Esalen writing teacher.

NANCY HOPKINS *These Are My Flowers* tracks a family story in Big Sur's rugged, innocent 1950s; text based on letters home.

HENRY MILLER A great literary sojourner. After Paris and Greece, Miller perched in Big Sur for 18 years, chronicled in *Big Sur and the Oranges of Hieronymus Bosch.*

ERIC BARKER Wild-haired British poet in a porkpie hat. Nepenthe regular. Died 1973. "Here we drink fog like rain."

JUDSON CREWS Texan poet and publisher, later Taos bookstore owner. Big hang-time with Miller led to two memoirs.

JOHN STEINBECK Salinas-born Nobel laureate, storied traveler, literary standard-bearer for Central California coast. Secret agent?

ELLA WINTER Left-wing journalist, co-founder of combative 1920s newspaper *The Carmelite* with husband Lincoln Steffens.

ROBINSON JEFFERS Poet renowned for his naturalist vision and fierce, stony language.

For an account of Big Sur settlement, see A Wild Coast and Lonely *by Rosalind Sharpe Wall. The Henry Miller Memorial Library is an excellent source of book recommendations suited to the landscape.*

THE ESSELEN TRIBE

The origin story of the Esselen people centers around Pico Blanco mountain, known in Esselen language as Pitchi.

When this world was finished, the eagle, the humming-bird and Coyote were standing on the top of Pico Blanco. When the water rose to their feet, the eagle, carrying the humming-bird and Coyote, flew to the Sierra de Gabilan. There they stood until the water went down. Then the eagle sent Coyote down the mountain to see if the world were dry. Coyote came back and said: "The whole world is dry." The eagle said to him: "Go and look in the river. See what there is there." *—A telling collected by Alfred Louis Kroeber, first anthropology professor at the University of California at Berkeley [and father of noted writer Ursula K. Le Guin]*

In an alternative version of the Esselen origin story, an eagle, a crow, a raven, a hawk and a hummingbird survive the flood. A feather with magic powers is plucked from the eagle and planted in the ocean to make the waters recede, re-creating the world.

The Esselen Tribe of Monterey County is not yet recognized by the federal government, but in 2020, the tribe regained a 1,200-acre ranch on ancestral land along the Little Sur River. esselentribe.org

STELLER'S JAY

Distinguished by its charcoal vest and brilliant blue wings and tail, the Steller's jay is an avian mainstay of Big Sur. Some call it a "blue jay," but that's conflating this bird, *Cynocitta stelleri*, with a distant relative. They forage, omnivorous and adept at storing seeds for winter, lifeways which make them seem oddly well-suited to Big Sur. And the sub-variety of Steller's jays here does bear a distinction: blue streaks on their black punk-rocker crests, unlike the white markings found inland. Like other corvids [crows, magpies, etc.], they are noted for their smarts and bravery; "attitude," it's even said. In the 1880s, writing of California's jays, Mark Twain opined: "[He] don't belong to no church, perhaps, but otherwise he is just as much a human as you be."

SHIPWRECK

San Francisco Call, April 23, 1894

HER LAST TRIP.

Wreck of the Steamer *Los Angeles.*
She Struck A Rock and Quickly Sank.

The steamship *Los Angeles,* bound from San Pedro to San Francisco, lies on the bed of the ocean in nine fathoms of water off Point Sur. Two of her passengers and one of her crew are known to have drowned, and five others are missing. The steamship struck on a sunken rock adjacent to Moro Rock and in full view of the lighthouse-keeper at Point Sur. The most conflicting accounts of the disaster and the loss of life are in circulation. The latest advices received from Monterey, forty miles to the north of the wreck, are to the effect that only four are known to have been drowned, and of these one body has been recovered. The whereabouts of five other men who were on the wrecked vessel is not known. They may have perished, or they may have reached the shore at some isolated spot. Point Sur has neither telegraphic nor telephonic communication with any other point.

THE FIRST NEWS.

Not Received Until Several Hours After the Wreck.

MONTEREY, April 22—Early this morning, John Gilkey, a farmer, living some twenty miles from here, brought the news that the steamer had made her last trip and was at that time at the bottom of the sea in the most rugged and rough stretch of the California coast. A party of citizens from here immediately started to render what assistance was in their power to the unfortunate people who had taken passage on the ill-fated boat. The steamer *Eureka,* going south, arrived here yesterday, and on its way down picked up several of the passengers of the sunken steamer, who had sought refuge on a raft. Captain H.D. Leland of the *Los Angeles* was among those on the *Eureka,* but to all questions asked him regarding the wreck he gave the same answer, "I don't know anything about it."

The difficulty in rendering aid to the site of the Los Angeles *disaster prompted the first proposals for a road through the region. Work on Highway* 1, *however, did not begin for more than* 20 *years.*

ADVERTISEMENT

Monterey Cypress, Saturday, September 10, 1892

SLATE'S HOT SPRINGS,
Below Point Sur, Monterey County, Cal.

The above named Springs are now open for the accommodation of the public.

Hot Sulpher Baths.

Beautiful Scenery, Lovely Climate, Good Hunting and Fishing, Etc.

Terms Reasonable.
Thos. B. Slate, Prop'r.

Thomas Slate originally claimed his hot springs property under the Homestead Act, as he pursued relief for his arthritis, and developed it into the Big Sur area's first attraction to travelers and seekers. Today, the property is home to the Esalen Institute.

HERMIT ENCOUNTER

California Coast Trails
Joseph Smeaton Chase, 1913

I came upon an original who for many years has lived a Robinson Crusoe life in a coign high up on the cañon wall. His ramshackle dwelling was more shed than house, and I found the ancient himself seated beside it, in a rather alarming state of undress. He was talking to himself as I approached, but hailed me hospitably to come in and sit down for a chat. His great topic was minerals, concerning which he had a theory, new to me, that every metal has a mother and a father. This great discovery had been revealed to him by an old Indian woman, once of these parts, who had bequeathed him a "map," by which, he declared, he was able to make his theory effective. To discount the palpable discrepancy between his apparently poor circumstances and his potential wealth, he explained that he cared nothing for actual money, being content with knowing that he could at any time procure it.

JOHN STEINBECK

John Steinbeck is a pillar of 20th-century American writing—and a global figure, as his 1962 Nobel attests. Still, California's Central Coast is his land: Monterey, his hometown of Salinas, the woods and shores of Big Sur. Steinbeck's descriptions fuse lyricism with salty reality to capture the towns and country, giving this part of California a permanent place in the world's canon of words.

FROM *CANNERY ROW*:

"Cannery Row in Monterey in California is a poem, a stink, a grating noise, a quality of light, a tone, a habit, a nostalgia, a dream. Cannery Row is the gathered and scattered, tin and iron and rust and splintered wood, chipped pavement and weedy lots and junk heaps, sardine canneries of corrugated iron, honky tonks, restaurants and whore houses, and little crowded groceries, and laboratories and flophouses."

FROM *EAST OF EDEN*:

"It was a deluge of winter in the Salinas Valley, wet and wonderful. The rains fell gently and soaked in and did not freshet. The feed was deep in January, and in February the hills were fat with grass and the coats of cattle looked tight and sleek. In March the soft rains continued, and each storm waited courteously until its predecessor sank beneath the ground. Then warmth flooded the valley and the earth burst into bloom—yellow and blue and gold."

FROM *TRAVELS WITH CHARLEY*:

"The years crawled back in their holes. It was the Monterey where they used to put a wild bull and a grizzly bear in the ring together, a place of sweet and sentimental violence, and a wise innocence as yet unknown and therefore undirtied by undiapered minds."

[On visiting the Salinas Valley] "I printed it once more on my eyes, south, west, and north, and then we hurried away from the permanent and changeless past where my mother is always shooting a wildcat and my father is always burning his name with his love."

"The vainest, most slap-happy and irreverent of men, in the presence of redwoods, goes under a spell of wonder and respect. Respect—that's the word. One feels the need to bow to unquestioned sovereigns."

MONTEREY INTERNATIONAL POP FESTIVAL

June 16-19, 1967
Monterey County Fairgrounds
Select performers and songs:

FRIDAY

THE ASSOCIATION .... "Windy"
LOU RAWLS .... "Love is a Hurtin' Thing"
JOHNNY RIVERS .... "Midnight Special"
SIMON AND GARFUNKEL .... "The Sound of Silence"

SATURDAY

CANNED HEAT .... "Rollin' and Tumblin'"
BIG BROTHER AND THE HOLDING COMPANY .... "Ball and Chain"
COUNTRY JOE AND THE FISH .... "I-Feel-Like-I'm-Fixin'-To-Die Rag"
QUICKSILVER MESSENGER SERVICE .... "Who Do You Love?"
STEVE MILLER BAND .... "Living in the USA"
MOBY GRAPE .... "Omaha"
HUGH MASEKELA .... "Society's Child"
THE BYRDS .... "Have You Seen Her Face?"
JEFFERSON AIRPLANE .... "White Rabbit"
BOOKER T. & THE M.G.S .... "Green Onions"
OTIS REDDING .... "Try a Little Tenderness"

SUNDAY

RAVI SHANKAR .... "Dhun in dadra"
BUFFALO SPRINGFIELD .... "For What It's Worth"
THE WHO .... "My Generation"
THE GRATEFUL DEAD .... "Cold Rain and Snow"
THE JIMI HENDRIX EXPERIENCE .... "The Wind Cries Mary"
THE MAMAS & THE PAPAS .... "California Dreamin'"

LILLIAN BOS ROSS

For many years, Eleanor Roosevelt wrote a nationally syndicated newspaper column called My Day. On October 9, 1942, the First Lady offered a short review of Lillian Bos Ross' novel The Stranger, *part one of a trilogy about a pioneer family.*

NEW YORK— I want to mention a novel called "The Stranger," by Lillian Bos Ross. A friend of hers, who is also a friend of mine, sent it to me. With it was a note from the author, from which I want to quote a few lines: "We Americans inherit stout boot straps, can pull ourselves up to victory. I was a homesteader's child, seventeen miles from the nearest log school. I didn't get to school, but I never gave up the idea that some day I would write books. This first book is my personal victory, and in troubled times, any victory is good." The story is laid in the very early California days and deals with the people who made good in the mountainous country of the Big Sur along that coast. It is coarse in spots, sometimes the attitude of the man towards his woman is almost unbelievable. Nevertheless, as a novel and as a character study, it holds your interest and carries a thread of inspiration all through it, which should be good for us in these days.

The Stranger *was adapted for the big screen in* 1974 *as* Zandy's Bride, *starring Liv Ullmann and Gene Hackman.*

CLINT EASTWOOD

The headline in St. Louis called it a "Fistful of Votes." In Pennsylvania, writers proclaimed, "No Punks in Carmel-By-the-Sea." Because in 1986, Clint Eastwood made national news for his most unexpected role yet—mayor of Carmel, California. The actor-director owned a restaurant in the heart of town at the time. Frustrated by rules around preservation and development, he ousted the incumbent, a retired librarian, with 2,166 votes for Dirty Harry Callahan and 799 for his opponent. "We're not interested in bringing in a lot of condos and hotels. There's plenty of them," Eastwood said on *CBS Sunday Morning*, a clip showing his attempts to assuage fears around his platform. He served a two-year term, a role that paid him $200 a month, before winning a Golden Globe in 1988 as Best Director for *Bird*.

ROBERT LOUIS STEVENSON

From "The Old Pacific Capital"

These long beaches are enticing to the idle man. It would be hard to find a walk more solitary and at the same time more exciting to the mind. Crowds of ducks and sea-gulls hover over the sea. Sandpipers trot in and out by troops after the retiring waves, trilling together in a chorus of infinitesimal song. Strange sea-tangles, new to the European eye, the bones of whales, or sometimes a whole whale's carcase, white with carrion-gulls and poisoning the wind, lie scattered here and there along the sands. The waves come in slowly, vast and green, curve their translucent necks, and burst with a surprising uproar, that runs, waxing and waning, up and down the long key-board of the beach. The foam of these great ruins mounts in an instant to the ridge of the sand glacis, swiftly fleets back again, and is met and buried by the next breaker. The interest is perpetually fresh. On no other coast that I know shall you enjoy, in calm, sunny weather, such a spectacle of Ocean's greatness, such beauty of changing colour, or such degrees of thunder in the sound. The very air is more than usually salt by this Homeric deep.

Stevenson, best known for Treasure Island, *spent time in Monterey and the region in* 1879. *The Stevenson House there continues to explore his legacy. The notion that he based his famed pirate novel on the area persists, though it's unconfirmed.*

REAL ESTATE

"BIG SUR DREAMING || Seeking Barn or Land"
Craigslist, 2022

Aloha if this message finds you. I am looking to make my dream come true in Big Sur. I LOVE LOVE LOVE barns and hold a vision of woodworking out in Big Sur. The trees and sea spark a light in my soul and I'd be honored to become part of your community. If you have extra land, I am looking for 1/2 acre or more, with or without a structure. I have 20k now and have excellent credit to continue paying a personal loan. I know its a long shot ... I am an artist who took a chance on love and lost my life earnings within one year ... Holding onto faith and praying for a miracle! Thank you for listening, sending big love!

HIGHWAY 1

"GREAT NEW HIGHWAY COAST TO OPEN SUNDAY"

The story of the realization of the San Simeon-Carmel link of the Roosevelt highway is the story of a titanic battle against almost superhuman odds. When this final section of the great coast route from Canada to Mexico is officially dedicated and opened to travel by Governor Merriam Sunday, a vision first dreamed forty years ago—which was to cost more than 8 millions dollars and take 15 long, laborious years before completion—will have become actuality. The work on the 93 miles between Carmel and San Simeon is heralded as one of the most noteworthy pieces of highway engineering on the west coast, and gives the traveling public a modern ocean shore highway of unparalleled beauty with superb views of the Pacific from elevations ranging from sea-level to that of Grimes point, 1058 feet above the surf. Construction has been accomplished by means of 38 contracts awarded by the state for grading, surfacing and bridges, and through the work of two prison labor camps which have been operating since 1928. *—San Luis Obispo Daily Telegram, June 26, 1937*

KEROUAC'S BIG SUR

Three comments on the novel written in '61, published in '62.

"In many ways, particularly in the lyrical immediacy that is his distinctive glory, this is Kerouac's best book. ... Certainly, he has never displayed more 'gentle sweetness.'"*—San Francisco Chronicle*

"On the surface, the novel has the random character of the early books: the hero has just been somewhere and is now going somewhere. [It is important to note that Beat travel is never really aimless. In *On The Road*, there is a good deal of talk about getting to Denver. Denver is not to be taken lightly.] In *Big Sur*, Big Sur itself is the first goal, and it represents a haven for the hero from his public self as King of the Beatniks." *—The New York Times*

"*Big Sur*'s humane, precise account of the extraordinary ravages of alcohol delirium tremens on Kerouac, a superior novelist who had strength to complete his poetic narrative, a task few scribes so afflicted have accomplished—others crack up." *—Allen Ginsberg*

SARDINES

The San Francisco Examiner
July 14, 1912

"MONTEREY SARDINES EATEN ALL OVER U.S."

California has given to the world so many gifts from her soil that the world is apt to forget she is a seaboard State. The gold from her mountains, the grains and fruits from her valleys, the oil and wine from her foothills, would seem almost to have run the scale of a country's resources. But California has the greatest ocean on the globe lying at her feet. It contributes to the wealth of California, in supplying her with sea food of an infinite variety. The handling of them is one of the great industries of the State. It remained for old Monterey, the cradle of California's greatness, to give direct from Neptune's table a delicious sea food which is becoming better known each year.

Six years ago some citizens of Monterey put up a packing plant and began to can the sardines. Each year has seen the plant grow as demands required. The product has met with much favor on this coast and also in the various Eastern cities where it has been introduced.

HOW SARDINES ARE CAUGHT

The sardine fishing is done mostly at night, the best catches being made in the dark of the moon. Any one who has been on the bay of Monterey on a night lighted only by the stars will remember the peculiar beauty of the waves tipped with phosphorescent light. This shimmering, shifting radiance comes from the myriads of little fish attracted by the boat's lantern.

After the night's catch the fishermen bring up at the cannery early in the morning. The fish are transferred to the salting and cleaning house on the wharf, where they go through a process of cleaning, scaling and washing, then up to the cooking rooms. Here they are laid in wire frying baskets and broiled in a vat of boiling olive oil until thoroughly cooked. As soon as they are sufficiently cooled, they are carried to the packers' tables and placed in the cans, into which the spices or sauce has been put.

By the middle of the afternoon the work of canning is done, the floors washed down, everything is scrubbed and quiet settles over the cannery wharf until the sunset hour when the fishing fleet again starts out to gather a new harvest.

ESALEN

The origins of a legendary retreat, center of deep thought and spur to "human potential."

In 1952, **RICHARD PRICE** graduated from Stanford with a sociology degree. Soon after, he joined the Air Force, assigned to San Francisco's East Bay. There, he roomed at the American Academy of Asian Studies, living with **ALAN WATTS**, an English writer delving into Zen thought and early counterculture vibrations. Price met the likes of Kerouac, Allen Ginsberg and poet Gary Snyder—core players in the Beat Generation drama. In 1957, he experienced a reported manic episode, though he emphatically denied that characterization, instead calling the moment "an attempt towards spontaneous healing." His parents committed him to a Connecticut mental health facility, where he was subjected to shock treatments.

In 1960, Price returned to San Francisco. Attending the Cultural Integration Fellowship, a spiritual center founded by Indian mystic Haridas Chaudhuri, Price met **MICHAEL MURPHY**. Murphy, also a Stanford man, had an eclectic philosophical background, shaped by professor Frederic Spiegelberg's comparative religions class, 18 months in an ashram in India, and a meditation experience on the banks of Lake Lagunitas. The two men hit it off. At the urging of author **ALDOUS HUXLEY**, they met Gerald Heard, founder of a Southern California experimental-thought center called Trabuco College. A pivotal four-hour conversation—evolutionary theory, biology, theology, philosophy—sparked an urgent conviction to found a new institute dedicated to expanding human horizons.

Two rules became mantras: "No one captures the flag" and "We hold our dogmas lightly."

They soon drove to a 375-acre property in Big Sur that Murphy's family had owned since 19 10, one-time Esselen tribal land. Murphy's **AUNT BUNNY** granted them a low-cost, long-term lease. In the fall of 1962, Murphy and Price presented the new Esalen Institute's first seminar series, **THE HUMAN POTENTIALITY**, based on a Huxley lecture. By the mid- 1960s, Esalen became a national byword for exploratory thought and liberated behavior.

ESALEN THINKERS OF NOTE

ALDOUS HUXLEY British novelist, best known for *Brave New World*. Thinking on "the human potentiality" gave Esalen early direction.

LAURA HUXLEY Upon 1963 death of Aldous, his wife took on many Esalen roles, including psychedelic experiments.

ABRAHAM MASLOW Coined "hierarchy of needs"; 1966 Esalen lecture expounded on "B values [Being-values]": goodness, beauty, uniqueness, justice, simplicity, richness.

JOAN BAEZ Led 1964 workshop called The New Folk Music, the first of seven Big Sur Folk Music Festivals.

FREDERIC SPIEGELBERG Stanford professor taught founders Murphy and Price; "religion of no-religion" merged Zen, philosophy, psychoanalysis.

ANNE WATTS Daughter of Esalen icon Alan and present-day teacher on joy, fulfillment, relationships.

FRITZ PERLS Creator of Gestalt therapy lived at Esalen [1964-1969] before leaving for Lake Cowichan, Vancouver Island.

SUSAN SONTAG One of the all-timers on glittering teaching roster. Along with Mailer, brought Soviet writers to campus in '70s.

STANISLAV GROF From 1973, developed "holotropic breathwork," a technique involving music, rapid breathing and other elements to induce altered states of consciousness.

GEORGE LEONARD West Coast editor of *Look* in 1960s, spearheading influential Institute coverage. Became Esalen's president.

ELLEN BASS American poet, author of *The Courage to Heal*, a self-help text co-authored with Laura Davis focusing on recovery from childhood sexual abuse.

IDA ROLF Creator of Structural Integration [a.k.a. "Rolfing"], an alternative medicine focused on alignment of the human body's energy field with the Earth's gravitational field.

For an in-depth history, see Esalen: America and the Religion of No Religion *by Jeffrey Kripal.*

VICTOR WONG

Jack Kerouac's novels teem with real people dramatized as players in his Beat-Generational chronicles. Among the walk-on characters, Victor Wong's turn in *Big Sur* provides a prime example of how Kerouac's orbit worked. A San Francisco Chinatown kid who spun a long and successful career as a Hollywood character actor, the real Wong becomes "Arthur Ma" in the novel. In the 1950s, during a time of study with Mark Rothko, Wong met Lawrence Ferlinghetti at City Lights Bookstore, site of Wong's first art show. That led to a call at Ferlinghetti's Big Sur cabin, and a meeting memorialized by Kerouac: "Arthur Ma ... never goes anywhere without his drawing paper and his Yellowjack felt tip pencils." Big Jack portrays Ma [who's sitting in Jack's chair, wearing Jack's hat!] as a vessel for the creativity of the times, churning out dozens of drawings, day after day. As Wong would later say at a tribute to the great novelist: "The time of the Beats was a time of celebration of the arts. Hey, in those days, the word was, 'Don't be a debutante. Don't dabble; plunge in. It's your bag, man, dig it.'"

HUNTER S. THOMPSON

Before he made "Gonzo" journalism his hallmark, the young writer from Kentucky served as an armed guard at Big Sur Hot Springs — formerly Slate's Hot Springs and the future site of the Esalen Institute. The experience produced one of Thompson's first major publications: a 1961 article on Big Sur's proto-countercultural scene for the pulp magazine Rogue *that hinted at his future style and perspective. A glimpse:*

"If half the stories about Big Sur were true the vibrations of all the orgies would have collapsed the entire Santa Lucia mountain range, making the destruction of Sodom and Gomorrah seem like the work of a piker. And, if justice were done, a whole army of tourists and curiosity-seekers would perish, too. It's not likely to happen, however, because almost everything you hear about Big Sur is rumor, legend or an outright lie. This place is a myth-maker's paradise, so vast and so varied and so beautiful that the imagination of the visitor is tempted to run wild at the sight of it."

MICKEY MUENNIG

The architect who defined a Big Sur aesthetic.

Unsung pioneer of California's organic architecture movement, Mickey Muennig created eco-designs that defined a certain very Big Sur look by integrating his buildings into the region's natural beauty. Following the wild coastlines, shaggy cliffs and shimmering seas, Muennig's designs cling to near-vertical drops and have rooms that cantilever toward the ocean. Muennig first arrived in Big Sur in 1971 after studying with the eccentric Bruce Goff, a friend and mentee of Frank Lloyd Wright. Soon after, he built his own home, a testament to his originality, with its glass doors and circular entryway facing the sea. Nicknamed locally the "White Elf" due to his stature and light hair, Muennig's magical creations included homes built partly underground [for temperature control], perched on stilts, or tucked inside a 22-foot-wide wine barrel. One of his most well-known designs for Post Ranch Inn is said to have no right angles. Muennig died in 2021, yet, if anything, his stature within architecture has grown as his legacy is assessed. His own Big Sur home, a bohemian otherworld of stone, wood and glass, went on the market for almost $8 million in 2022.

PEBBLE BEACH

Three vintage U.S. Open performances at the legendary public golf course

NICKLAUS 1972 In the first Pebble Beach Open, big blond Jack uses his 1 iron to launch a famous shot on the 17th hole. The ball pings the flagpole, drops dead for an easy putt.

WATSON 1982 Tom Watson, chasing Nicklaus, faces a tricky shot out of rough grass on 17. A delicate chip, a sweet roll, and Watson takes a boyish victory lap around the green.

WOODS 2000 Lacking in drama but not dominance. Tiger Woods commands the field start to finish, breaking numerous records, including the best-ever Open round at Pebble.

HENRY MILLER

Born in Brooklyn in 1891, the writer Henry Miller spent nearly a decade in Paris as an expat, cultivating free expression and the bohemian life of pre-War Europe. When Miller arrived back in the United States, many of his books, forthright on sex and other subjects, were deemed obscene and banned in here. Then, during an uninspiring 1944 stint in Los Angeles, a friend invited him to Big Sur. He was, he wrote, hooked by the wide-open space and the "grandeur and eloquent silence."

Miller found inspiration in Big Sur's "skies of pure azure and walls of fog," a description included in his 1957 memoir, *Big Sur and the Oranges of Hieronymus Bosch*, published as his underground reputation as a literary touchstone and model of artistic rebellion grew. Some say his writing about presence spurred early tourism in the area, as well as the Beat generation's interest in Big Sur.

Miller left Big Sur to return to Paris in 1963, just a year before the Supreme Court rejected a Dade County, Florida, ban of his book *Tropic of Cancer*, still one of the most censored books in history. The justices voting to lift the ban—Black, Douglas, Brennan, Stewart and Goldberg—cited the reasoning in a case against an Ohio movie theater [*Jacobellis v. Ohio*] that spawned the infamous line by Justice Potter Stewart regarding obscenity:

"I shall not today attempt further to define the kinds of material I understand to be embraced within that shorthand description; and perhaps I could never succeed in intelligibly doing so. But I know it when I see it, and the motion picture involved in this case is not that."

The liberation of Miller's writing came to be seen as a watershed First Amendment moment. When Miller died in 1980, *The Guardian* wrote:

"As chief literary anarchist of his day, a kind of low priest celebrating the last rites of what he regarded as a doomed civilisation, it was not surprising that he became a hero of the Sixties beat generation."

The Henry Miller Memorial Library ["Where Nothing Happens"] is home to collections of Miller's work and other papers, and hosts an eclectic variety of music performances and other events.

BIG SUR HOUSES OF NOTE

TOR HOUSE Robinson Jeffers' place is a monument to his craggy, nature-obsessed poetry. The stone: handhewn. The lights: candle and oil from 1919 to 1949. The name comes from the rocky promontory that also bears Hawk Tower, the retreat Jeffers built for his wife, Una.

GEORGE BROOKE-KOTHLOW'S BIG SUR HOUSE In 1992, a California architect known for idiosyncratic modernism nestled a summer home into Big Sur's hillsides. Adobe-wrapped hidden treasure.

COASTLANDS HOUSE Stacked patios with vast views wrap behind sliding glass panels. Rugged stone walls offset sleek interiors. A design by noted architects Carver + Schicketanz.

BURNS CREEK HOUSE A heavy 1967 groove in salvaged parts by Lloyd Kahn, eco-architecture forerunner, geodesic designer and shelter editor for *Whole Earth Catalog*. Railroad ties, farm-camp lumber.

FALL HOUSE Oft-photographed cliffside stunner by architect Anne Fougeron. Runs long and narrow, tracing the landscape down. Clutch use of a cantilever.

BUTTERFLY HOUSE In 1951, architect Frank Wynkoop sketched a midcentury masterpiece on the Carmel oceanfront, named for its roofline that looks set to take flight.

HEARST CASTLE Monument to Gilded Age power, hubris, vision and skill, funded by legendary mining and media tycoonery. Career high-water mark for architect Julia Morgan.

SAM TROTTER HOUSE Trotter, early Big Sur legend and tanbark trader, hammered out a rambly cabin years before Highway 1. Today, a vine-draped stronghold of whimsy.

THE GLASS HOUSE Mickey Muennig's half-whimsical, eco-minded vision is Big Sur's architectural touchstone. The late architect's own pad: glass-domed sleeping areas, *Dwell* mag splash when it went on sale of late.

D.L. JAMES HOUSE A stony-walled compound in Carmel Highlands, slung low and inspired by a Cornish castle, is a 19 18 winner from Arts an Crafts master Charles Sumner Greene. Recently hit the headlines for its new owner: Brad Pitt, actor.

THE CARMEL PINE CONE

"CARMEL HAS NEW NEWSPAPER"

Carmel, historic Carmel, down on the Monterey peninsula, has a new weekly newspaper, of which one Overstreet, formerly a clerk in the post-office, is presiding genius. Overstreet's introductory editorial, his salutory, contains some startling announcements, many of them new and original. Among them is noted, "We have come to stay," and "This paper is here to fill a long-felt want." However, Overstreet qualifies his expressions by relating that he has come to stay as long as the general public and the business interests of Carmel prosper or suffer him to remain, to which he adds: "To permit this journal to struggle and languish—and mayhap die—would be a far greater loss to the community than to the publisher." All of which seems to have touched a popular chord, for one leading resident remarks that the advent of the paper is the beginning of a new era. So mote it be. The new sheet is called "The Pine Cone" and will be celebrated for its " 'pinions." —*Oakland Tribune*, February 9, 1915

The Carmel Pine Cone *is still going strong and can be perused remotely via* pineconearchive.com.

TRENT REZNOR

A note on an alt-rock star's Big Sur reverie.

Big Sur's reputation as creative muse perhaps rests on older big names—Steinbeck, Jeffers—but its lure extends into more modern days. The leading man of '90s angst standard-setters Nine Inch Nails repaired here after years of hard touring, seeking only to write music. It proved, word is, an emotionally trying time. Reznor left with one song, "La Mer." Its sparse lyrics—originally in French Creole, oddly enough—testify to the same world of stone and surf that inspired so much famed creativity of the past: "When the day arrives, I'll become the sky, and I'll become the sea."

SPIRITUAL CENTERS

Essayist, novelist and travel writer Pico Iyer was once quoted in a New York Times *article about retreats in Big Sur—centers like New Camaldoli Hermitage, which Iyer has been known to visit—to the effect that such places are for people who "crave a kind of peace, an active quiet and a silence that isn't merely the absence of noise, but the presence of a kind of quickening. A place to do what is hardest, which is nothing at all."*

NEW CAMALDOLI HERMITAGE
Contemplative community and home to 16 Benedictine monks, amid 900 acres off Highway 1. Visitors can book day trips or longer retreats.

TASSAJARA ZEN MOUNTAIN CENTER
Drive 14 miles up a dirt road near Jamesburg to the first Zen monastery established outside Asia. Spanish American name derives from Indigenous Esselen, meaning "place where meat is hung to dry."

LAND OF CALM ABIDING
Tibetan Buddhist center for serious Dharma students, near San Simeon. Two-room cabins for short retreats [one month] or longer. Located on 525 acres, it's all silence and space.

THE KEELING CURVE

A Big Sur-born landmark of scientific concern.

The Big Sur coast is known for its ocean science, but discoveries here extend high into the atmosphere. Many scientists credit the "Keeling Curve," named for Charles David Keeling, with revealing the problems of excess carbon dioxide in the atmosphere. Keeling camped at Big Sur sites in the 1950s, tracking carbon with measuring devices he created himself. Soon after, he tested levels in Antarctica and on Mauna Loa, Hawai'i. In 1960, he published "The Concentration and Isotopic Abundances of Carbon Dioxide in the Atmosphere" in the international scientific journal *Tellus*. At the time of his initial research, scientists imagined most carbon dioxide would be absorbed naturally, and did not think carbon emissions could have a notably harmful effect. Keeling's track of rising levels over time has been called one of the most important scientific works of the 20th century.

ROBINSON JEFFERS

The poetic voice of a rugged shore.

Born in Pittsburgh, son of a Presbyterian minister and Old Testament scholar, Robinson Jeffers [1887-1962] was destined to be a fierce voice. The Big Sur coast would be the land where that voice found its shape. After childhood schooling in Europe, he studied classics at Occidental College, and literature and languages at the University of Southern California; he also dallied with medicine and forestry along the way. Friendship, an affair and her divorce led to a marriage with Una Call Kuster in 1913. The couple settled in Carmel, a bohemian refuge, where in 1916, Una gave birth to twin sons. A few years later, Jeffers bought land on Carmel Point, apprenticed himself to a stonemason and began building Tor House, the family's dramatic home. Soon he also started work on Hawk Tower, a retreat on the property he named for a hawk that accompanied him as he pulled stones up from the sea. [The day the project ended, the hawk departed.] Amid all this labor, his poetic voice emerged, lean, grounded and much like the buildings he made. ["My finders had the art / To make stone love stone."] Jeffers would call his aesthetic "inhumanism," his work a call to focus on nature and its great forces: the beauty of sea, stone, sky, and the freedom and ferocity of wild animals. This vision made him one of the most famed and influential poets of his era, his suitably craggy profile appearing on the cover of Time in 1932. Never sentimental and often uncompromising, Jeffers' lines echo the waves crashing against the rocks of the coast he called home.

ARTICHOKE QUEEN

"Members of the Salinas Kiwanis club cheered loudly yesterday noon at their meeting in the Santa Lucia Inn as Randy Barsotti of the artichoke association pinned an orchid and banner on Miss Marilyn Monroe, 20th Century-Fox starlet, who has been nominated Artichoke Queen. Miss Monroe was a guest of the club during the meeting, and was not only introduced to the local brand of artichokes, but met many of the local growers. Feature of the regular weekly luncheon was a talk by the Rev. Ed Bowling, who paid tribute to the memory of Abraham Lincoln. Rev. Bowling, whose father was one of Lincoln's many friends, gave members an insight into the religious and moral side of the great president."
—The Californian, *Salinas, February* 20, 1948

NORA MAY FRENCH

"Between Two Rains"

It is a silver space between two rains;
The lulling storm has given to the day
An hour of windless air and riven grey;
The world is drained of color; light remains.
Beyond the curving shore a gull complains;
Unceasing, on the bastions of the bay,
With gleam of shields and veer of vaporing spray
The long seas fall, the grey tide wars and wanes.

It is a silver space between two rains:
A mood too sweet for tears, for joy too pale—
What stress has swept or nears us, thou and I?
This hour a mist of light is on the plains,
And seaward fares again with litten sail
Our laden ship of dreams adown the sky.

Nora May French was a poet associated with Carmel's vibrant early bohemian community, who wrote often of the California coast. She died by suicide in Carmel in 1907 at the age of 26.

LANDSLIDE

"FAMED HIGHWAY LEADS NOWHERE"
The Californian, March 9, 1983

World famous Highway 1, ravaged by fierce storms, now dead-ends in Monterey County. The needed repairs on the highway are so difficult and numerous that travel between Los Angeles and San Francisco is unlikely for many months. In the Big Sur area, the highway will be closed to tourists for months while temporary repairs are completed. Nature keeps changing the timetable. Tuesday night, a quarter-mile wide mudslide buried Highway 1 at the north end of the Big Sur Valley, south of Andrew Molera State Park. Residents again are cut off and without electricity. It will be at least a day before a makeshift road can be dozed through the muddy ooze.

BIG SUR FOLK FESTIVAL

Los Angeles Free Press, September 19, 1969

The steep incline from Highway One at Big Sur leveled abruptly and there was the Festival amidst a cluster of buildings on a sweeping lawn. In front of the lawn was a pool surrounded by a handsome slate deck. Behind this pool, the Pacific Ocean, lazy and quiet, glass-like under a carpet of kelp. At the rear of this pool, there were four painted canvases hung as backdrops, a stage setting for the annual Big Sur Folk Festival.

This past weekend in alternately chilly and warm weather and under overcast skies, some of American's best contemporary musicians performed, at the Big Sur Folk Festival, a romantic musical idyl by the sea. For two days thousands lay about the Esalen Institute's spacious grounds, caught up in the gentle atmosphere, delighted in each other, the setting and the performers as well.

There were no battalions of cops ducking squadrons of flying wine bottles at this festival. There were no enemies, only friends.

The festival's formal music presentation began when Joan Baez led the Festival's cast of performers into the staging area from the midst of the audience singing "Swing Low Sweet Chariot" and "O Happy Day" as she proceeded, the audience standing and clapping time.

The stage area cleared and Baez started to sing. The audience joined in as she sang "I Shall Be Released" making it a hymn. It was the first of many sing-alongs she would initiate throughout the Festival.

Joan Baez, in and out of the crowd—on stage with her guitar—with Dorothy Morrison—with Mimi Farina—then again with her Mountain Resistance Band. She was accompanied throughout the weekend by Steve Stills, by John Sebastian. Singing a cappella, her voice echoing back from the hills above, was both eerie and beautiful when she sang "Carry It On" in a voice surprisingly strong and sure.

Joan Baez, sounding a warm greeting to the kids lining the road above watching free, then speaking about what her draft resistor is experiencing in jail, [horrors and all] proudly saying he has not been rehabilitated. She sang as well as I have seen her sing before but with more joy and less sorrow in her reading of lyric. More than any other, her presence and voice dominated the Festival. She set the mood.

The 1969 *edition of this short-lived festival* [1964-1971]
is documented in the film Celebration at Big Sur.

CROPS

ARTICHOKES State vegetable thrives in Castroville's fog. Andrew Molera, state park namesake, credited as early planter.

STRAWBERRIES Traditionally Monterey County's top crop: worth $922M in 2020. Spring rains hit hard in '22.

LETTUCE Salinas, "Salad Bowl of the World," faces a number of insect, fungal threats. State researchers seek solutions.

CAULIFLOWER Monterey County grows about half the Cali caulies, total, and the state in turn produces half of America's supply.

WINE GRAPES Newcomer among CA's designated winegrowing regions: San Luis Obispo Coast, stretching toward Big Sur.

BRUSSELS SPROUTS Salinas is America's brussels epicenter, and 1,200-acre Ippolito is a powerhouse grower.

CELERY A top-10 crop in Monterey, worth $146M in 2021. Canada is a major consumer.

SPINACH In 2019, Salinas-based Agricultural Research Service unveiled USDA Red, antioxidant super-dose.

GARLIC Will Rogers on Gilroy, inland from Monterey Bay: "The only town where you can marinate a steak by hanging it on the clothesline."

MUSHROOMS Wild porcinis thrive in region's pine forests; Monterey Mushrooms is a brand of national heft.

RASPBERRIES An up-and-coming crop here, thanks to perfect growing conditions and strawberry market saturation.

CANNABIS Legend tells that an unnamed monk bred Big Sur Holy Bud strain in 1965. Too good to fact-check.

With more than 7,000 acres, El Sur Ranch comprises about 12 percent of the Big Sur region's private land. It has operated as a cattle ranch since 1834, its original deed issued by Mexican authorities.

INCLUDED

066 *Foundations*

067 *Ecosystems*

068 *Ed Ricketts & Kelp Forests*

069 *Sea Otters*

070 *Wildlife Watching*

071 *Monterey Bay Aquarium*

072 *Deep-Sea Creatures of Note*

074 *Research Vessels*

075 *A Working Scientist*

076 *Perspectives*

PURSUIT

A field guide to the study of ocean science in the Big Sur region, from its historical roots to an iconic aquarium to the creatures, landscapes and vessels of the deep, deep sea

OCEAN SCIENCE

The sea's currents, underwater geology and weather combine to make the waters off the Central California coast some of the richest in the world. Accordingly, the region is a major hub of marine research—work that often weds exploration, engineering and conservation.

FOUNDATIONS

GEOLOGY Beneath Monterey Bay, where the ocean takes a bite out of the land just north of Big Sur, lies a chasm whose proportions rival those of the Grand Canyon. The largest submarine canyon on the Pacific Coast, its main channel meanders for nearly 300 miles before petering out on the abyssal plain. Formed by fast-moving "turbidity currents"—essentially, underwater avalanches—the canyon's shape is ever-changing. More than a mile deep in spots, it offers researchers unusually close-to-shore access to deep-sea habitats.

HISTORY Early European visitors described bounteous wildlife. Boom-and-bust cycles of exploitation quickly followed. Sea otters, prized for dense pelts, were hunted nearly to extinction. Whalers fired explosive bomb lances at migrating grays and humpbacks. Even seabird eggs were harvested to feed hungry gold miners. During the sardine boom of the 20th century [see *Cannery Row*], Monterey Bay fleets hauled out about a million pounds of the small, silvery fish each day—and dumped so much putrefying offal that tourists fled en masse. But this, too, was short-lived: by the late 1940s, catches plummeted and the sardine industry collapsed.

RECOVERY & CONSERVATION Once the canneries closed, Monterey Bay began to cleanse itself. In the 1960s, sea otters paddled back in. Their return was crucial: absent these voracious eaters, urchin populations had grown unchecked, decimating kelp forests in the process. Now aquatic jungles could recover, providing habitat to fish and invertebrates—a buffet for seabirds, sea lions and seals. Since it opened in 1984, the Monterey Bay Aquarium has been a standard-bearer for conservation. And in 1992, Congress designated more than 6,000 square miles of Pacific as a national marine sanctuary, vital protection as threats to ocean health—from warming to acidification to plastic pollution—multiply.

ECOSYSTEMS OF THE CENTRAL COAST

SANDY BEACHES A habitat constantly remade by waves and wind. Thumb-sized crabs, bristle worms and itty-bitty, seaweed-munching crustaceans known as beach hoppers burrow into the sand for protection. Western snowy plovers nest in shallow nooks right on the beach.

ROCKY SHORES As tides roll, animals and plants live with extremes: submerged, exposed, battered by the surf. Intertidal zones play home to snails and chitons, sea stars, self-cloning anemones, spiky sea urchins and a droopy-mouthed fish called the monkeyface prickleback.

COASTAL WETLANDS Salt-tolerant pickleweed, pencil-thin pipefish and great blue herons thrive in muddy, low-lying marshes and estuaries. Bat rays, leopard sharks and sea otters give birth in these shallow waters, which also provide an important stop for migrating birds in spring and fall.

KELP FORESTS Giant kelp grows from rootlike holdfasts on the rocky sea floor to form luxuriant canopies at the ocean surface, towering up to 175 feet tall. Here, biodiversity soars. Invertebrates—brittle stars and sea stars, sponges, anemones, tubelike tunicates, urchins—dwell at the bottom. Rockfish, buoyed by gas-filled swim bladders, hover in the understory. Gray whales, seals and sea lions shelter beneath the canopy. On the surface, sea otters coil themselves up in kelp fronds to avoid bobbing away at naptime.

OPEN WATERS The vast pelagic zone is home to the microscopic [plankton, basis of the ocean's food chain] and the colossal [the blue whale, the largest animal on earth]. Jellies pulse gently as sea turtles power through the water with paddlelike flippers. Sardines and anchovies, meanwhile, dart and swirl, schooling as a defense against predators that include sharks, dolphins, whales and seals.

DEEP SEA The planet's largest ecosystem features little to no light, near-freezing temps and enormous pressure—and yet plays host to more species than any habitat on land. This is the little-studied domain of bioluminescent jellies and fanged fish, a world where giant larvaceans build mansions out of mucus and bone worms feast on whale skeletons on the seafloor.

ED RICKETTS

The inspiration for Doc in John Steinbeck's Cannery Row, *Ed Ricketts was a real-life philosopher-scientist and pioneering ecologist who filled his Monterey lab with specimens from the intertidal zone: the dynamic area where land and sea meet. In 1940, he wrote:*

"Who would see a replica of man's social structure has only to examine the abundant and various life of the tide pools, where miniature communal societies wage dubious battle against equally potent societies in which the individual is paramount, with trends shifting, maturing, or dying out, with all the living organisms balanced against the limitations of the dead kingdom of rocks and currents and temperatures of dissolved gases. A study of animal communities has this advantage: they are merely what they are, for anyone to see who will and can look clearly; they cannot complicate the picture by worded idealisms, by saying one thing and being another; here the struggle is unmasked and the beauty is unmasked."

Ricketts' 1938 book Between Pacific Tides *remains a touchstone for tide pool lovers.*

KELP FORESTS

A key sanctuary for ocean creatures faces environmental threats.

As complex as their counterparts on land, kelp forests are one of the most biodiverse ecosystems on the planet. Giant kelp can grow up to two feet per day, forming hundred-foot-tall algal cathedrals that support hundreds of plant and animal species. Until recently, kelp forests thrived up and down the California coast. But since about 2013 they've been in decline, hit hard by a marine heat wave—kelp prefers cold water, which is much richer in nutrients—and a mass die-off of sunflower sea stars. The disappearance of this keystone predator left sea urchin populations to boom, and the spiky purple echinoderms chewed their way through kelp holdfasts. Now so-called "urchin barrens" carpet entire swaths of the seafloor. [Able to endure starvation mode for decades, the animals are essentially zombies.] This isn't just bad news for marine life: kelp forests capture up to 20 times more carbon than forests on land, so they play a powerful role in mitigating climate change. One spot of good news: while forests farther north have virtually vanished, in Monterey Bay, healthy patches remain thanks to the presence of urchin-loving sea otters.

THE SOUTHERN SEA OTTER

Select field notes on Enhydra lutris nereis.

1. This adorable mustelid once ranged from Baja to Japan, the entire northern Pacific Rim. The southern sea otter is one of three subspecies.

2. With the densest pelt in the animal kingdom—up to one million hairs per square inch otters were nearly exterminated by fur traders seeking "soft gold." In California, they were believed extinct.

3. In 1938, about 50 otters—a group at rest is called a raft—were spotted near Bixby Bridge in Big Sur. Since then, they've expanded along roughly 300 miles of the Central Coast and now number about 3,000.

4. One of the rare mammals to employ tools, otters use rocks to crack open clams, crabs and mussels while floating on their backs. They may hold onto a favorite rock for a while, tucking it into a pocket of loose skin.

5. Otter pups are born with such buoyant fur that they float like corks, but mothers will still wrap them up in kelp fronds for protection.

6. As a keystone species, otters play an outsize role in their ecosystems, which in California include kelp forests and estuaries. Otters keep invertebrate populations in check, which helps the whole system thrive.

WILDLIFE WATCHING

Where and when to observe the coast's exceptional diversity.

ELKHORN SLOUGH RESERVE

One of California's few remaining coastal wetlands, this 7-mile tract of tidal salt marsh just inland from Monterey Bay harbors an abundance of wildlife, including more than 100 sea otters. They're here year-round, but spring is pupping season [it is for the harbor seals too]. Also in the mix: barking sea lions; smoothhound sharks, gliding through the shallows; hundreds of species of birds, resident and migratory. Stroll the reserve's 5 miles of trails, rent a kayak or stand-up paddleboard from an outfitter in Moss Landing, or book a tour on a pontoon boat.

PACIFIC GROVE MONARCH BUTTERFLY SANCTUARY

Right at the tip of the Monterey Peninsula sits one of the largest winter sites for monarch butterflies in North America. From November to February, thousands of the brilliant orange pollinators seek shelter among the eucalyptus, pine and cypress trees. They're best visited during the early afternoon hours, when they spread their wings to the sun.

POINT LOBOS STATE NATURAL RESERVE

These rugged headlands at the northern end of the Big Sur coast offer choice cetacean viewing. Gray whales, which travel close to shore, pass twice on their migration: in winter, from late December to early February, they head south to breed; they return come spring, between March and May, with calves in tow. Over the summer months, spot humpbacks performing acrobatics. Blue whales, whose spouts top 30 feet, also slide by in summer and fall. Dolphins, porpoises and orcas make appearances too.

PIEDRAS BLANCAS ELEPHANT SEAL ROOKERY

Just up Highway 1 from Hearst Castle, thousands of elephant seals hang out on a sliver of sandy shore. Though they can be seen galumphing across the beach year-round, winter brings birthing and breeding, which means adult males fighting for mating rights by flinging their blubbery bodies [which weigh up to 5,000 pounds] at one another and trumpeting through their pendulous, inflatable proboscises.

THE MONTEREY BAY AQUARIUM

The story of the region's defining research center.

In the 1970s, Cannery Row was a carcass of its former self. Monterey's sardine boom was decades past, and abandoned oceanfront factories were rotting into the sea. One of them, Hovden Cannery—once one of the Row's largest—was owned by Stanford University. Purchased to create a buffer zone next to the school's marine lab, in practice it mostly served as a place for scientists to party on Fridays. Four of those scientists had a notion: What if they transformed Hovden into an aquarium devoted to the coast's biodiversity? [This idea was off-trend at the time: American aquariums preferred tropical fish to tide pools.] Fortuitously, the group also had the connections to make it happen. One of them, Nancy Burnett, was a daughter of Silicon Valley entrepreneur and engineer David Packard, who'd been looking for a new project to fund.

By the time Monterey Bay Aquarium opened in 1984, the Packards had poured in $55 million. Though much of the building was unsalvageable, architects preserved the old boilers and smokestacks. The warehouse, its floor littered with sardine can labels, became offices. The pump house, originally built to pull in fish from floating wooden tanks in the bay, was redesigned to draw raw sea water at a rate of 2,000 gallons per minute, 24 hours a day. From all perspectives it was a project tremendous in ambition and scale, requiring the efforts of engineers and set designers, fiberglass artists and artificial rock-work artisans. For the now-iconic kelp forest exhibit, the first of its kind in the world, Packard himself drew up a design.

More than two million people visited the first year. A wing was added later for a million-gallon open-sea exhibit, and most recently, the aquarium opened a $ 15 million exhibit showcasing rarely seen marvels of the deep sea. Education, research and conservation are central, from jelly breeding to sea otter rescue. A sister organization, Monterey Bay Aquarium Research Institute [MBARI], unites marine-science research with cutting-edge technology [a current focus: ocean health].

But none of this, says Julie Packard—another daughter of David, and the aquarium's executive director since it opened—comes at the expense of the aquarium's most potent calling card: sheer wonder. The ocean covers 70 percent of the earth's surface and yet remains poorly understood. So to glimpse the mysteries of the deep, Packard says, "gets your mind above the human condition for a while."

DEEP-SEA CREATURES OF NOTE

Thousands of feet below the ocean's surface, remarkable life-forms thrive.

GIANT ISOPOD

Example of deep-sea gigantism—the tendency of deep-sea animals to grow large—this colossal crustacean cousin of the pillbug can be bigger than a football. Bottom-dwelling scavenger; may go years without eating.

BLOODYBELLY COMB JELLY

Wears crimson for camo [red disappears in the deep sea] and propels itself with tiny cilia that become glittering ladders of iridescence as light diffracts and refracts. Excretes sparkly dung.

SEA ANGEL

Inch-long swimming sea snail known for mesmerizing swishing of wings. To feed, it pushes hooklike tentacles out of its head to pry other snails from shells, then swallows them whole.

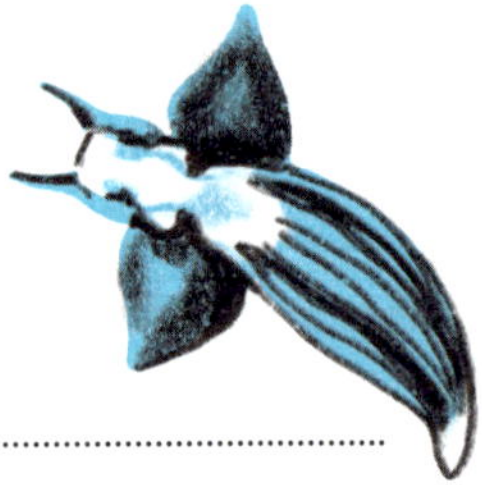

FLAPJACK OCTOPUS

Resembles lumpy pancake while resting on seafloor. Pulses through water on webbed arms while flapping stubby fins. So cute scientists considered calling it *adorabilis*.

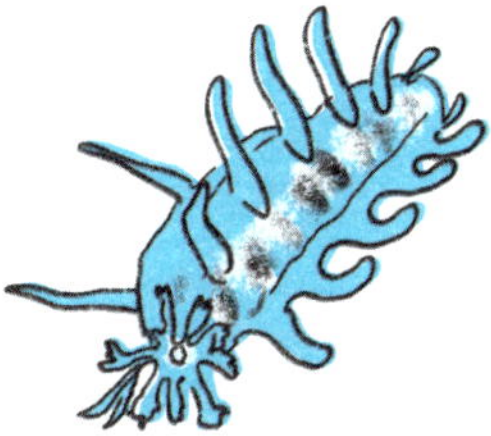

SEA PIG

Pink-tinged, translucent sea cucumber. Crawls across the abyssal plain on elongated tube feet, using 10 tentacles encircling its mouth to root in mud for a dinner of decaying animals and algae.

BLACK SEA DEVIL ANGLERFISH

Ambush predator. Bioluminescent pole on head functions as a glowing lure to prey, which are quickly inhaled into gaping mouth and trapped behind long, sharp teeth.

BARRELEYE

Sports upward-facing, bright-green eyes in a transparent dome, allowing the fish to scan for silhouettes of prey swimming overhead in the water column. A wee thing, up to 6 inches long.

BASKET STAR

Baroque relative of the brittle star. Intricately branching arms are lined with tiny hooks, helping this filter feeder catch plankton and small crustaceans.

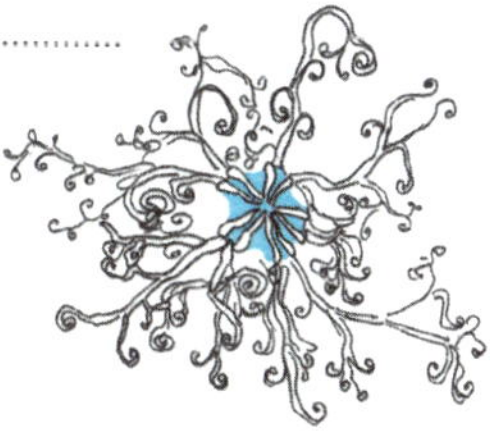

BIOLUMINESCENCE

Three quarters of deep-sea creatures in Monterey Bay make their own light. This chemical reaction serves a variety of purposes, from creating camouflage to luring prey to deterring predators to attracting a mate.

RESEARCH VESSELS

WESTERN FLYER

John Steinbeck and Ed Ricketts put in six weeks and 4,000 miles on this 76-foot purse seiner—a Monterey Bay sardine boat, with keel and decking of old-growth Doug fir and ribs of white oak—on their 1940 expedition to the Gulf of California, a voyage detailed in *The Log from the Sea of Cortez*. Currently under restoration for use as a floating classroom.

R/V DAVID PACKARD

Fully operational in 2023, the Monterey Bay Aquarium Research Institute's flagship vessel will hold 12 crew members and 18 scientists.

ROV DOC RICKETTS

This MBARI vehicle is an unmanned robotic submarine the size of a minivan. Tethered to the ship where its pilot sits, it can dive to 2.5 miles, with high-def video cameras and sampling equipment.

BENTHIC ROVER II

Collecting data as it crawls along the muddy seafloor, this autonomous rover—the size of a small car—aids in MBARI's long-term monitoring of the deep-ocean carbon cycle.

A WORKING SCIENTIST

MacKenzie Bubel—Monterey Bay Aquarium colleagues call her "Bubbles—is fueled by fascination for the creatures of the deep. The aquarist on her places of work and research:

THE JELLY LAB "It's basically a nursery," Bubel says: more than a thousand tanks and mazes of tubes, where Bubel and others breed and care for jellyfish. Lacking brains and bones, many begin life as polyps, stuck to the bottom of a bin that Bubel likens to a seed bank. Production is on-demand: when the aquarium needs more, scientists adjust water conditions [temperature, say, or salinity], and polyps produce larvae.

IN THE WATER Every night, droves of marine life rise from the deep, the largest synchronous migration on Earth. "At the advent of radar, they thought it was fish," Bubel says. "But it's really all tiny planktonic organisms cruising hundreds of meters, every single night, to chase food, to spawn at the surface and then come back down to safety for the daytime hours." To witness vertical migration firsthand, Bubel's taken after-dark scuba trips—a.k.a. "blackwater dives"—in Hawaii. A favorite creature? The larval-stage slipper lobster. "They're so laterally compressed they're like a little see-through potato chip," Bubel says. "They have legs that swim and legs that grab. Sometimes, they'll carry tiny box jellies around and use them as whips, in defense. Everything is so tiny but so vicious."

ABOARD SHIP Bubel has also served as chief scientist on MBARI expeditions. Steaming into Monterey Bay, the team drops a minivan-sized remotely operated vehicle into the submarine canyon below. This science robot operates high-def cameras and collecting equipment designed for fragile gelatinous life. In a control room, Bubel trains her eyes on video screens as a pilot guides the robot. "They make it look so easy. There's currents going this way, the boat's going that way, and they're like, 'You want that tiny see-through thing? Yeah, no worries.'"

ADVANCED READING

The Extreme Life of the Sea *by Stephen R. Palumbi and Anthony R. Palumbi: A marine biologist father and writer son examine backward-aging jellyfish, worms dwelling in scalding hydrothermal vents, more.*

PERSPECTIVES

"We were on humpbacks yesterday. What they do in Alaska, the humpbacks release bubbles in a stream. The bubbles, as they rise, help concentrate the small schooling fishes. The whales were so focused on it. When they exhaust the air, you can smell the krill they're feeding on. It's a full scratch-and-sniff immersion exhibit. But you don't have to go in a boat—it's right off the deck of the aquarium. Yesterday we had sea lions and dolphins going by. From our restaurant people have watched orcas come in and kill seals. To be plopped down in this marine environment, it's as close a reconnection to nature as we can get."
—**JOHN O'SULLIVAN**, director of collections, Monterey Bay Aquarium

"I was out on the Duxbury Reef at Bolinas, right north of San Francisco. It's fantastic tide-pooling. Everybody was looking at the critters, and nobody seemed to be talking about what I was seeing the most of. I held a scrap of seaweed up to the sky, and was blown away by its color and form and shape. One of the astounding things about seaweed is that it's not all green, and even when it is green, it's a really beautiful shade of green. The sea lettuce is classically kelly green, because it only has chlorophyll in its chloroplasts. But the red seaweeds are vibrantly red, from magenta to purple to orange, and that's because they have red and blue accessory pigments in their chloroplasts to collect different wavelengths of light. And the kelps have a brown accessory pigment, and that mixes with the green to make this array of golden colors and olive greens and deep browns. Then there's this incredible diversity of forms, from feathery to these thick blades that are almost like denim. The red seaweeds are kind of stretchy, even. There's a tactile quality that is so appealing."
—**JOSIE ISELIN**, artist and author of *The Curious World of Seaweed*

"We have greater access than we've ever had for the oceans. We have greater understanding about some of the ecological issues and sensitivities, how the climate is affecting ocean conditions, evidence about how that might be affecting ocean life. There's tons of hope about our ability to change the trajectory—the arc of ecological doom—to an arc of ecological hope. We can now think hard about protecting wild spaces, being much more prudent about our approach to extracting deep-sea resources, whatever they are, from minerals to biology, and think not what can we get but what can we save and maintain and benefit from, those freebies, those ecological services the ocean provides."
—**JIM BARRY**, scientist, Monterey Bay Aquarium Research Institute

INCLUDED

080 *Magnus Torén*

083 *Carol O'Neil*

084 *Gary Griggs*

085 *Anne Fougeron*

087 *Martín Palafox*

088 *Kirk Gafill*

090 *Eric Keener*

093 *Laura Mckinnon*

094 *Catherine Mulligan*

096 *Bree Harlan*

INTERVIEWS

Ten conversations with locals of note about literature, camping etiquette, lighthouse history, family legacy, foraging, weddings, architecture and more

MAGNUS TORÉN

DIRECTOR, HENRY MILLER MEMORIAL LIBRARY

BIG SUR IS a place where it is okay to get lost. It's okay to feel a little scared. It's okay to feel that we are alone out here in this big wilderness.

WHEN I FIRST came to the United States, it was 1977 in the wintertime. I'm from Sweden, which is why I have an accent

I CAME UP from the Caribbean into New York, spent three amazing months in New York City, then jumped on a Greyhound bus and came to San Francisco.

I SAW BIG SUR the first time as I hitchhiked down the road in the spring of 1978.

MY LIFE WAS very interesting. I was sailing on sailboats. In 1984, I delivered a sailboat back from Fiji to San Francisco.

I DIDN'T HAVE anything to do particularly, so I took a job at Ventana, the hotel, because I thought Big Sur was such a beautiful place.

THE SENTIMENT and physicality of the landscape becomes paramount for almost anyone. That's the main attraction.

AND THEN I meet a young woman on the highway one day, and I have a motorcycle accident and she helps me recover from the motorcycle accident. And she's still my wife.

A FEW YEARS LATER, I walked into the Henry Miller Library. The person who was working there said, "I'm going to quit this. I don't want to do this anymore." And I said, "I'll do it."

HENRY MILLER LIBRARY has been this little funky wooden cabin that defends its right to be a little funky. A little spontaneous. A little unplanned, perhaps.

WE HAVE a steady stream of wonderful people from all over the world stop by.

THE OPEN MIC, it has been incredibly good, in terms of vibe and camaraderie and being

Peace

together, and then also good in the quality of the performances.

THAT'S NOT REALLY the main ambition, but it's fun also when people sound really good.

WE HAVE TO be careful with being too popular.

THERE'S A LOT of projection on what people want Big Sur to be. There are articles from 1959 in *Life* magazine about playing music in the afternoon, having a yoga gathering on your front porch, going hiking with a poetry book in your back pocket.

THERE IS, of course, truth to that part. But it's certainly not the only thing here.

NOW MORE THAN ever, the northern part of Big Sur has become a hangout for the very, very wealthy.

IN THE SOUTH part, it's more of a mixed bag. Some people work for the government. Some old remnants of the hippie homesteading culture.

NOT EVERYBODY can write the great American novel.

YOU WAIT TABLES and do whatever you can.

SOMETHING YOU CAN do, something else to grow. Figure out something to sculpt.

DOWN IN THE South Coast you have people working with jade, doing jewelry.

THE COMMUNITY ITSELF gathers around. We gather around the community health center, the local fire brigade.

SPEND TIME AND really soak it in. Stop at the turnouts.

BREATHE IN THE ocean air. Look at the incredibly beautiful meeting of land and sea.

MAYBE GET INTO a little bit of a meditative mode, about where you're from, where you're going and what's going on in your life.

IF YOU ARE lucky enough to come here at night and drive the highway, stop and turn off all your lights. Sit there for at least 20 minutes. Then look up.

WHEN THE SKY is good in Big Sur, it is better than any sky I have seen in all my sailings around the world or hiking in northern Sweden.

THE MILKY WAY is like a white cloud.

CAROL O'NEIL

LIGHTHOUSE HISTORIAN

WE'VE LIVED IN Monterey 28 years. My husband's a retired marine colonel, and we owned our house here from when he was a student at the Naval Postgraduate School. So we came back to Monterey.

BIG SUR—well, it's probably the most beautiful place we've ever been in the world, and we've been a lot of places. It's just ... Is "magical" too trite a term?

I JUST KIND of fell into the historian thing.

WE SAW AN ARTICLE on Point Sur Lighthouse, so we went down and took a tour, and they sucked us right in.

IT'S ALL VOLUNTEER staffed, everything except law enforcement and the porta-potties.

POINT SUR WAS identified as a place for a lighthouse in 1866. Shipwrecks on the coast hustled it long. They turned on the light in 1889, and it has been in continuous operation since then.

IT'S ONE THING to be on the coast. It's another thing to be slightly off the coast.

POINT SUR IS almost an island out there. You see the mountains and the coast. On a clear day, you can see all the way to Santa Cruz.

I'VE BEEN THERE in January, with whales going past and it's 72 and sunny. And I've been there in July, with howling winds and fog. I always take a sweatshirt.

THE DIRIGIBLE *Macon* wrecked in 1935, right off of the lighthouse, off the rock. Pretty astounding.

WE HAVE ALL this gee-whiz GPS technology. But if it goes out for some reason, a light will tell you where you are. It's an actual thing, a tangible fix.

SHIP CAPTAINS TELL me they still look forward to lighthouses.

"YES, I'M ACTUALLY in the right place." Something they can count on.

GARY GRIGGS

GEOLOGIST

ONE OF THE nice things about Big Sur is it's just wild. It tells you, "Here's what can happen."

IT'S DIFFERENT from living in Dallas or Los Angeles, where you're pretty much controlling everything. Here, you don't control very much at all.

BIG SUR WAS formed by plate collision. Part of the Pacific went down and pushed up this stuff onto the coastline.

WE HAVE STEEP slopes, unstable rocks. We get pretty frequent fires, and once you burn off the vegetation, we can get these torrential rainstorms.

I HAVE A photograph that my father took in 1956, perhaps, of our old station wagon pulling a little trailer with all this gear on it in Big Sur.

MY FATHER WENT to college at Berkeley in forestry. He ended up teaching high school math, but for him, getting out in the redwoods and camping was fun.

I WENT TO UC Santa Barbara, because I was surfing and my brother was there. I thumbed through the catalog and found geology.

I DID OCEANOGRAPHY in grad school—marine geology, the undersea geology—and then came to UC Santa Cruz. I just finished my 54th year of teaching here. I couldn't have asked for a better profession.

THE SOIL and all the burned stuff is unstable. Down it comes.

IT'S NOT BECAUSE the geologists or engineers are incompetent. It's young geology that's still evolving, so there's nothing we can do.

WE CAN JUST keep putting Band-Aids on it.

BIG SUR, it really isn't a destination. It's a path.

EIGHTY MILES OF incredible landscape that you have to slow down and enjoy.

ANNE FOUGERON

ARCHITECT

WE'RE AN architectural firm in San Francisco, which I started in about 1986 and still run. We do a lot of different projects, but often single-family homes on unique, complicated sites.

WE ALWAYS TALK about the poem by Wallace Stevens: "I placed a jar in Tennessee."

IF YOU PUT a man-made object in a natural environment, both the object and the landscape are transformed by their presence together. For better or worse.

WHEN WE FIRST started working on Fall House, we called it "the banana slug."

IT'S ABOUT THE IDEA that you put a building on the site that completely follows the topography.

THE SITE WAS very limited in size. The client wanted to have views from most of the rooms. And the only way for us to do that was a building that kind of cascades down the hill and faces out north.

I REMEMBER getting an email from the client saying, "Hey, would you be interested in doing a house here?" And it was a picture taken from the ocean, looking back on this site. And I was like, "Yeah, sure. I'll do that. No problem. Thanks."

IT'S A SPECTACULAR 200-foot-tall sheer wall of granite going right into the ground.

IT'S ALSO THE violence of the ocean as it eats at the cliff edge.

SO YOU'RE SEEING both the ocean and the cliffside together—a relationship I really like—opposed to just looking at a horizon of the sea.

IT'S BEEN PUBLISHED widely, in things like *Architectural Record*, on the cover. A bunch of different books. In a bunch of photo shoots.

IT WAS AN exceptional, rough site with an iconic enough shape that it was easily recognizable. It doesn't look like anything else.

Post Ranch Inn

MARTÍN PALAFOX

COMMUNITY LEADER

I MOVED IN 1980, '81. That was when Highway 1 washed out. You could only go out one day, and come back the next day.

VENTANA, when I got here, I would say they had a Hispanic population of 20. This place was not even born. I mean, you can count back then.

I WAS PROBABLY, what? 17? This is my hometown. We're from Jalisco, but when I go out there, I miss this place. I go to LA, I miss this place.

THE FIRST YEAR when we got here, it was a lot of hippies. Man, they're still here, right? Good people. They were always hitchhiking down south, and you picked them up and they rode in the back of the truck. You could still have that then.

THESE DAYS, if you got somebody in the back of your truck, you're in trouble, right? Not in those days.

I STARTED AT Post Ranch, 1990. We did all the undergrounds, working with Mr. Post. We opened in '92.

THE HISPANIC COMMUNITY, it grew up so fast in the '90s.

BASICALLY, at the first stage, it was landscaping and hospitality, which is the couple hotels and the restaurant.

PRETTY MUCH everybody who lives here and works here has multiple jobs.

WE DON'T HAVE a mayor. We have the CHP. We have a sheriff. That's it.

BUT IF YOU see somebody's doing the wrong thing, I will say so, or somebody else does.

WE UNDERSTAND THE rules that Big Sur has. Keep it. Save it. Don't trash it.

EVERYBODY understands what Big Sur is. There's one way in, one way out. Respect each other, because we know each other.

KIRK GAFILL

OWNER, NEPENTHE

MY GRANDPARENTS started Nepenthe in 1949.

MY TITLE IS president. CFO. I'm also the general manager. I'm the third generation, working with my mother, the second generation.

MY GRANDPARENTS' goal was to find property to raise their five children on. It wasn't to create a business.

TOURISM WAS NOT only not a global phenomenon, it wasn't even a local phenomenon. It was people coming down for hiking or hunting, in a much smaller context in terms of numbers.

THE INITIAL CONCEPT was just to do a very simple hamburger stand. A roadside attraction.

A FRIEND OF theirs was an architect named Rowan Maiden, a student of Frank Lloyd Wright's. Their whole social circle had this incredible array of artisans and artists.

ROWAN CAME UP with the design—much more ambitious. That's what they ended up doing. They built the restaurant in a remarkably short time frame.

OPENING DAY was this wild success. My grandfather thought, *Oh, my God. We're an overnight hit.* He went out and bought all the supplies he could possibly come up with. Nobody delivered back then. You had to manage all of your own needs.

THE NEXT DAY, maybe 10 people showed up.

THEY DIDN'T HAVE a phone on the property for years. The first phone was the payphone that we have on the stairway.

JUST GENERATION after generation of drunk, crazy chefs coming through. Then, of course, in the '60s and '70s, it was absolutely the dropout PhDs.

BOHEMIANS TO beatniks to hippies. Big Sur was right in the midst of it—the gathering places, the watering holes. Then Esalen. All of these things were happening in the same time and place.

I GREW UP on the property. From when I was 10 years old, I worked a different job every summer. I learned all the nooks and crannies of the business, all the way through college.

EVEN TO US, it felt like a very remote backwater.

I REMEMBER my grandmother's black-and-white television. ABC seemed to come in fairly well. NBC was a blur. CBS, you got nothing. In high school, kids would be talking about a show on CBS, and I never knew what they were talking about.

I ALWAYS THOUGHT this would be a second career. Maybe in my 50s or 60s, when my mom retires or something along those lines.

MY MOM HAD a situation where she had a medical emergency where she was out of work for about six months.

IN THOSE EARLY years, I was still really torn. I thought, "This is not where I'm supposed to be. I should work for General Motors or IBM or something, or be in politics in DC."

THEN ABOUT two or three years into that, I just said, "Either leave and go do those, or make yourself happy."

I ALWAYS feel my grandmother saw that this would be eternally in our family. Many, many generations. I thought, *Okay, I love that idea.*

I'M VERY ATTRACTED to old-world stories. Winemakers that go back to the 16th century, very connected to a particular place in the world—this sense of soil and place and artisanship.

I'VE TRIED TO envision where we can go, how to achieve that. In the simplest sense, I can at least contribute to making Nepenthe as successful as possible. Not just in a dollar sense, though that has to be a big part of it, but in ways that represent the values my grandparents had.

WHEN YOU'RE HERE, you realize how incredibly resonant the experience has been for so many generations.

MY SON IS working today. That's fourth generation.

ERIC KEENER

OCEAN FORAGER

YOU CAN MAKE an entire bouillabaisse out of stuff you collect in tide pools, from rock crabs to owl limpets.

I WAS A PRO motorcyclist. I got heavily into snowboarding. We moved to Pacific Grove, and it made sense to hop in the water.

WHEN YOU free dive, you're holding your breath. I found it less an adventure sport, more an opportunity to meditate, almost.

YOU HAVE TO slow your heartbeat down. You've got to just float there. Be okay with the currents, the waves, the animals, the kelp columns all around you.

THE MOMENT YOU start to dip underwater, everything goes away.

MY STATIC BREATH hold is about four and a half minutes.

I BECAME A spearfisherman, and started winning competitions. And then I decided that killing animals for points in a competition was kind of weird.

FIN + FORAGE is a brand about ocean conservation. We started a new type of competition that focuses more on food, less on the catch. Now they're throwing catch-and-cook competitions in Australia and San Diego.

FOR ONE PROJECT, we descended a 300-foot cliff in Big Sur, then swam an Olympic distance while we hunted for food.

WE MET ONE of our chefs on a private beach, and made arguably the best meal that's ever been cooked at the ocean.

ROCK SCALLOPS cement themselves to rocks and cracks underwater. You have to take what's basically a tire iron. Dive down, holding your breath, and exert huge amounts of energy trying to pop a scallop off a rock.

THEN, COME BACK up before you drown.

I'LL JUST POP off one of the shells while I'm in the water and eat the bud. So tasty.

LAURA MCKINNON

YOGA TEACHER

ALL LIFE, IN many ways, could be considered yoga.

WHEN I WENT to my first yoga retreat at Esalen, it wasn't just the retreat itself. It was something very much connected to that piece of land.

THE MINUTE I arrived, it just captured me.

ESALEN HAS ITS own garden. So when you eat meals there, you're eating food grown on that land. You can taste the service and the heart that goes into growing it.

WHEN YOU ARRIVE, there's a long, steep driveway down. The whole property sort of sits below the highway.

EVEN IF I'M only there for five or six hours, I feel a distinct difference when I come back to the top of the driveway and meet Highway 1.

IT'S JUST SUCH a removal. You can forget the rest of the world and focus on whatever it is you're looking for down there.

I HAVE LED daily movement classes. When people are there for workshops, they can participate in other activities. An early morning yoga class, generally at 7:30, is one of those.

KNOWING THAT I would be meeting people from all over the world, I would try to weave in different themes—something would inspire me on my drive down, or just something from what's happening in my life at that moment.

WHAT I APPRECIATE most about Esalen is that whatever you're looking for to feed your heart, feed your soul, feed your spirit, you will find it.

IT OPENS UP the doorway to your inner self.

FOR DEEP DISCOVERY within yourself. Finding the answers that have been sitting in your heart all this time.

CATHERINE MULLIGAN

EVENT PLANNER, BIG SUR BAKERY

IT'S NOT EASY to live in Big Sur. It seems like it would be, because it's so beautiful. But there are all sorts of sacrifices people make.

ANYBODY WHO'S working and sharing something, you already know it's really important to them.

I WAS WORKING in the yachting industry before I moved here. My résumé said I wanted to work on an "environmentally friendly boat." That doesn't really exist—there aren't environmentally friendly yachts.

I LOOK AROUND Big Sur, and it's like, "Okay, this is it." You do, in the funniest ways, get exactly what you wanted.

BECAUSE BIG SUR does feel a bit like an island. You are so isolated. If you aren't environmentally friendly in Big Sur, Big Sur will just spit you right out.

WE ARE FOCUSED on making the dish meet the ingredient where it is, rather than forcing ingredients into the dish.

IT'S NOT GOING to be watered down, or try to taste like something else.

OUR CHEFS AND cooks, they came from lots of fast-paced, strict kitchens, putting out beautiful, tweezered-out food. And that level of culinary delivery is still here. But we're more focused on sourcing the freshest, most unique ingredients from the Central Coast.

THE POSTS WERE some of Big Sur's first homesteaders. Their daughter, Alice Post, had an idea for a succulent and cactus garden right at the edge of the highway. Big Sur Bakery is in the house she and her husband, Steve Jager, built.

I'LL GET EMAILS that say, "We want to have our wedding at Big Sur Bakery because we came in for a bacon bow tie in 2017, and we've been dreaming about it ever since."

THE BACON bow tie actually looks almost like a puff pastry, twisted, with a large strip of bacon inside it.

IN MY JOB, I work with lots of couples. It's just such an epic place. It reaches that level of love without having to add too much.

WITH PROPOSALS, IT'S like a five-minute event. So you have five minutes to make it right. With weddings, I talk to both halves of the couple, and it's not a surprise anymore.

IN 2020, it was my first fire season in California. I was totally freaked out. But anytime I saw someone with the Big Sur Volunteer Fire Brigade, I was just like, "Thank you for keeping us safe. Thank you for sharing the right information."

THEN I LEARNED one of the girls at the bakery, Sarah, is also a firefighter.

SHE BRINGS HER pager with her to work as a server. She has her firefighting uniform in our staff room, ready to rock.

EVERYBODY KNOWS WHEN the pager goes off, you say, "Thank you. I've got you."

THE WORD "BIG" in Big Sur—it really is like a big experience. A big view of the horizon.

THE JAW-DROPPING sunset. The way the sun shines through the redwood trees.

THE SQUAD OF turkeys walking you to your car. There's always something when I open my eyes.

SOMETIMES the space—Big Sur itself—will present a challenge. A change in the weather, or the road's closed, or natural disasters.

THE PLAN OR timeline is completely derailed because of some *thing* that's only in Big Sur.

IT'S JUST SOMETHING that sounds wild, because it is wild. It's definitely the wild.

BREE HARLAN

SOUTH COAST ADVOCATE

I WAS BORN and raised at Lucia, about 25 miles south of Nepenthe.

THE SOUTH COAST is a lot more remote—a little less cohesive than the North Coast. People live up in the mountains and in smaller communities.

I'M SORT OF like an unofficial city council representative. Even though there isn't really a city of the South Coast of Big Sur, I sort of represent people down there at this point.

THERE IS ACTUALLY a bit of a crisis. The Forest Service is understaffed for the number of visitors.

THE NUMBER ONE thing would be to discourage people from expecting to have a campfire. We're in the middle of a 1,200-year drought.

AND THEN, come prepared for the eventuality that if you're going to have to go to the bathroom, there are no public bathrooms. Bury your toilet paper at the very least.

IT'S ALL OFF the grid. There's no PG&E down there. Anybody who lives down there is either on a generator or solar power. There's no infrastructure besides the highway.

THEY'RE THE KIND of people who know how to troubleshoot a solar array or an inverter when it's acting up. Very self-reliant. It takes a special kind of person.

MY FAMILY HAS lived at Lucia since 1870 or 1890 or something.

MY DAD'S KIND of a mechanical genius. It's not unusual to go over to his house and find half a transmission in the bathtub.

I LOVE BIG SUR in all its seasons. I love it when it's pouring rain and the roads are crumbling and flooding. I love it in the summer when the mountains are covered in gold grass and it's hot as hell. I love it when you're up on the mountains and the air is dry and it smells so good.

INCLUDED

100 PERMISSION TO ENTER
By Jedidiah Jenkins

107 DOC'S LAB
By Leslie Williamson

113 FIVE POEMS
By Robinson Jeffers

STORIES

Essays and selected writing by noted voices from Big Sur and Highway 1

PERMISSION TO ENTER

Written by **JEDIDIAH JENKINS**

BIG SUR will always be remote. The cliffs are too steep, the mountains clustered enough to make travel permanently inconvenient. One day, when we all have personal hover-drones to take us wherever we want to go, perhaps then Big Sur will change. Until that happens, its difficulty is its charm. The southern slopes bake in the sun and stay mostly grass. The northern slopes, relieved of the sun's heat, hold the fog longer and give redwood trees, oak trees, blackberries, poison oak, and every other plant a chance to grow thick and gnarled. And in the meeting of every mountain is a stream, or sometimes a decently big creek, that scrubs the boulders bald and gurgles and pools into crystal-clear oases. Red salamanders stand out in the gray-and-green world of the creeks. The steepness of the ravines makes these microclimate forests dark. Redwood bark and evergreen richness and sharp oak leaves. These dark places feel like a secret. And they keep secrets.

For centuries, there have been rumors of "dark watchers" in these forests. On the ridges of the mountains. In the distance. I've read that the Spanish explorers saw them, calling them *los vigilantes oscuros*. Robinson Jeffers acknowledged them in poetry: "forms that look human to human eyes, but certainly are not human. They come from behind ridges and watch." Even John Steinbeck mentioned them, in a short story called "Flight" published in 1939. "Pepé looked suspiciously back every minute or so," the story goes, "and his eyes sought the tops of the ridges ahead. Once, on a white barren spur, he saw a black figure for a moment, but he looked quickly away, for it was one of the dark watchers. No one knew who the watchers were, nor where they lived, but it was better to ignore them and never to show interest in them. They did not bother one who stayed on the trail and minded his own business."

I love a local legend, bespoke to the environment and energy of a place. The dark watchers of Big Sur *feel* true. They feel appropriate to the shadows cast by the steepness, by how vertical the distances are, how you can stand on a ridge and gaze out, the miles playing tricks on the eyes. You feel as if you could fly.

* * *

I have been camping many times in Big Sur, and I have been in those shadowy places, and once, I made contact. Or something like that. It went like this:

A group of my friends from Los Angeles and San Diego picked a weekend in October to drive up and camp in some of the national forest just up the mountain from PCH. Up a dirt road where the camping is free and primitive. We found a dense forest with a big opening perfect for our trucks and jeeps to circle up, set up chairs, get some burgers grilling and beers flowing. We've come to that site for years because it is almost always open, gorgeous, and a short hike goes down to a flowing creek cradled in boulders. There were six of us, mostly married men excited for a boys' trip and no crying babies. I was the lone gay, single man, and these straight boys seemed to love it. We sat in our circle, getting properly drunk and talking, all in the purity of isolation from our phones. Our little fire lit our faces but left the forest and the world beyond us to darkness.

At an advanced hour—maybe midnight, I'm not sure—we heard a voice at the edge of the woods.

"Permission to enter your camp?" the voice said.

A man. A voice that wasn't one of us.

He had a heavy smoker's raspiness, with a concerning tone. You can tell so much about a person from tone. He had a performative sincerity mixed with Adderall alertness. A neighborliness and charm that sounded like lying. We looked at each other quickly with excited glances, and we said, "Yes." He emerged from the dark. He had crispy blonde hair coming out from a beanie. His face was very tan and his smile lines were deep enough to fit a nickel. He wore an oversized hoodie, jeans and Vans. I couldn't tell his age. A very rough 35 or a damn good 65. His accent was almost comically Southern Californian. He had several rocks in his hands.

"I've never seen you guys before. First time to Big Sur?" he said.

"I've been here a bunch, been to this spot a couple times. I usually stay up at Kirk Creek," I said.

"Kirk Creek is beautiful. Well, welcome to the forest," he said, opening his arms in a gesture of bestowing. "I'm a jade collector. A jade expert. I've spent the last eight years collecting jade in these creeks and shaping them and selling them." He handed us each a piece of jade, cut into the shape of a fat arrowhead. I worried he was about to try and sell them to us.

"Hold it up to the light, it'll glow green," he said. "I want you to have these. As a welcome gift to the woods."

"Wow, thank you!" my friend said.

"Yeah, man, jade saved my life," said the man. "I was in the Gulf War, and I came back screaming at the sky every night, yelling at the big man. I woke up with Jack Daniels and mushrooms. I wasn't killing myself quick enough. I looked down one night on the ground and saw a stone and picked it up and realized that there was still beauty in the world, and I started that day looking for it. It saved me from my mind. One guy once said to me, 'I will beat the shit out of you,' and I said, 'You won't do half as good of a job as I have done to myself.' "

"Do you want a beer? Whiskey?" I asked him.

"Oh man, I gave that up. But I'd take a cigarette if you've got one.'

I fished in my backpack for some and handed him a few. He was very happy.

* * *

This man from the woods felt weirdly fitting for a Big Sur experience. The place fosters mystery. Every time I've come here, I feel a pull to the strange and mystical. The way people talk about Sedona and Santa Fe as being vortexes—I don't know if I believe in all that, but I must say I do feel something in Big Sur. I don't really think rose quartz and jade have "power." But for some reason, certain places on this planet attract people. Not people looking to get rich or raise a family, but people looking to commune with energies otherworldly.

In 2013, I was cycling from Oregon to Chile. Near the beginning of my trip, I passed through Big Sur. It was then I really felt the layered realities of the place. I was run off the road by RVs from Ohio and thick clots of tourists at every vista and bridge. But the Henry

Miller Library, Deetjen's, the forests and creeks we camped by—all told a different story, the story of a town where real people live. But people deeply informed by place. This isn't a man-made world, where the affairs of culture and society are on the tongue. It is a place where Big Sur is always being discussed. A rockslide. A fire. A destroyed road.

The tourist comes through and gobbles up a view. The local lives in constant conversation with land and place and change and the way things were.

* * *

"This world is crazy, man. I moved here eight years ago to run from the cops. I got a jaywalking ticket, and I was like, *Screw that.* So I moved up to the woods.

"My dad was Mr. Universe, a real famous body builder; he won the title at 18, and again at 72. I grew up at Little Dume, in Malibu. I traveled, I made big money, but I blew it all. I was on acid for a year and a half. I think the Universe—God—took my money from me. I always wanted to do right by God, but I gave him 99 percent and kept 1 percent for me. I thought it was a secret. I lived for God, but then finally I realized I was really living for the 1 percent that was mine. I told God and He laughed at me and said, 'You think I didn't know!' Ha!"

"Hey, you haven't even told us your name," I said, hoping that basic social convention might override his waterfall of words.

"I'm sorry. I'm Viking. Been called Viking for many years."

"Viking? Is that your real name?" I asked.

"No. But no one calls me my real name. It's Richard. I changed my name because the government wants me for the jaywalking ticket. So I usually don't tell anyone my real name. Not sure why I just told you guys, but screw it. I'm happy you're here."

I thought to myself: *They must want him for more than jaywalking.*

My friend Jason chimed in. "Do you find us city kids coming into your woods annoying?"

"No. I don't own this. No man owns anything. It's just borrowed. This nature is too beautiful for just me or these old timers. And nobody owns anything. It's just as much yours as it is mine. And I've had it for so many years, I consider myself blessed. I've spent so much time in these woods. Too much. I went a year and a half without seeing one person, man. Not one. I started talking to the animals. When I would walk through the woods, at first the birds would call to each other to warn about the dangerous animal coming their way. But now, the birds don't warn. They know me. But I was talking to the birds and the trees, and the problem is when the trees start talking back. Loneliness is the worst cancer."

Certain things he would say landed like heavy wisdom. I thought about how lonely he was, and how he knew it. How playful his language was, even funny, and how so much of who I am is formed by how I fit in with friends and family and strangers and community, and what would happen to me if I didn't have that.

"You know, when I got here, I thought there was nobody in these woods. But I just didn't see them. And they hid from me. Like the warning birds. There's a lot of us living in these creeks. People everywhere. If you see trees, there's people in there, and they know you're here. But we're good people. And the jade is always so good to me. You know a guy in China just bought a jade stone for a billion dollars."

"A billion dollars?" my friend Brady exclaimed.

I knew that couldn't be true. It would have been front page news if a stone sold for a billion dollars. But I was liking this guy, and I have never been one to correct strangers or new friends.

His words kept flowing. "I see you guys have smart phones. You know the government is watching you, right? All the time. They can listen in on your phone whenever they want. But I don't give a shit. My computer, I don't care. I won't even walk in front of my computer unless I'm butt naked with peanut butter and jelly on my chest. *Watch me*, I say. *I'll give you a show*."

* * *

Three hours passed. Viking had gone through all our cigarettes and wasn't showing any signs of slowing down. He was talking about the history of the PCH and waving his hands, dramatically uplit but the fire, when I caught the eyes of a few of the other guys. *Ding*. The internal timer hit its limit.

I interrupted: "Okay, Viking. We're gonna head to the redwood circle and listen to a podcast. We've been planning on it. Thanks so much for visiting. I feel like we've seen a side of Big Sur from a local we would never have known. You're amazing." I hoped complimenting him would make the severing easier. He was snapped back into seeing us and knowing where he was.

"Oh yes, of course, thanks so much for the cigarettes and the time, men. I'm glad to have you in these woods." He stood up, and we hugged. "The jade is yours. It will guide you," he said with a bow, and he stepped backward and bowed again into the black wall of the dark. He was out of sight. He was gone.

We've gone back to that spot many times, but Viking has never returned to us. As much as we like being together and left alone, there is a strange sense of loss with that: a feeling that we aren't worthy of a watcher anymore. Like we're getting older and closing ourselves off from mystery and weirdness.

I look at the narrow ravines between mountains differently after Viking. Thinking of the dark watchers. Folklore often springs from exaggerated truth. The forest is not empty. The redwoods are huddled up, whispering old things. And the shadows are watching. No place is really empty. There is no blank canvas waiting to be conquered by tourists or settlers. Every place is swarming with birds and life and, yes, people. Viking had it right. He asked permission. And with a little investment, soon the birds stop chirping a warning and receive you.

JEDIDIAH JENKINS has written two *New York Times*-bestselling memoirs, *To Shake the Sleeping Self*, about cycling 14,000 miles from Oregon to Patagonia, and *Like Streams to the Ocean*. He is the cofounder of Byta, making travel mugs designed to promote a reusable economy.

DOC'S LAB

Written by **LESLIE WILLIAMSON**

A FACTORY STEAM WHISTLE still blows at noon every day on Cannery Row, its sigh as much a nod to the street's former life as the heart of Monterey's sardine industry as it is theater for the aquarium visitors who largely people the street today. When I first heard that whistle, I was tucked in a sky-blue 1930s bungalow, not far away, on a writing deadline for my fourth book. My writing schedule tends to be monastic—eat, write, sleep, repeat—with the occasional fall down a research rabbit hole. But that steam whistle, marking my time as it would have if I had lived 100 years earlier, sparked a curiosity that made me veer off from my desk to explore.

Growing up an hour away in the San Francisco Bay Area, Monterey was not a place I ever visited, just a town I drove through on my way to Carmel, which interested me far more for its artist-colony past. I had vague bits of historical knowledge—John Steinbeck's *Cannery Row*, the aquarium opening to fanfare in the mid-1980s—but not much else. So I did as I always do in a new place: I went looking for the old places. We leave a part of ourselves in the spaces we live, love and spend time in—a soul print, if you will, and these are the places I seek out. That's what took me to 800 Cannery Row, a ramshackle building sandwiched between two old canneries, one now a hotel, the other a souvenir shop.

It's a flat-roofed, weathered wood building with a row of windows looking down on the street. Originally, it was a single-story home for a family of sardine fishermen, complete with curing tanks in the backyard. In 1928, it was purchased by a marine biologist named Edward Flanders Robb Ricketts to house his company, Pacific Biological Laboratories, and eventually himself and his family.

Ed Ricketts was, by all accounts, a magnetic personality in real life. But it's Steinbeck's portrayals of him on the page that created the cult-like status that surrounds him and this humble building to this day. Steinbeck turned Ricketts into the *Cannery Row* character "Doc," and collaborated with the scientist on the explorations recorded in *The Log From the Sea of Cortez*. If the connection to the famous author saved Ed Ricketts from being obscured by time, that's no more than he deserved.

He was, by and large, a self-taught marine biologist. He worked outside of academia, making ends meet by selling biological specimens—frogs, cats, marine invertebrates, et cetera—to schools and labs. As he collected specimens for his business, he observed and studied the marine life of the shore, called the intertidal zone. These studies culminated in the 1939 book *Between Pacific Tides*. Today, the book is seen as a foundational text for marine biology and ecological thinking. When it was published, its focus on the web of relationships between different species was ahead of its time.

This sensibility, his way of observing relationships between living things and their environment, colored the way he navigated his own life as well. Ricketts is remembered as being kind to others regardless of station in life—nonjudgmental, a great listener, a bit of a ladies' man. His home, on what was then called Ocean View Avenue, was a meeting place for friends—remarkable, when you consider what his neighborhood must have smelled like, surrounded by a couple dozen sardine canneries, and more remarkable still for the cast of characters around Ricketts: composer John Cage, writer Henry Miller, local artist Bruce Ariss, mythologist Joseph Campbell and, of course, Steinbeck and his wife Carol. All would hang out into the wee hours to drink, philosophize and listen to whatever music happened to be playing on Ricketts' old phonograph. [His taste ran to Bach, Lead Belly and Gregorian chants.]

There is today no separating Ed Ricketts from Steinbeck. "Doc would listen to any kind of nonsense and turn it into wisdom," Steinbeck wrote in *Cannery Row*. "His mind had no horizon—and his sympathy had no warp. He could talk to children, telling them very profound things so that they understood. He lived in a world of wonders, of excitement."

This life of the mind and senses ended tragically, just three days before Ricketts' 51st birthday. While running out to get steaks and salad for dinner, his old Buick was hit by the Del Monte Express train a few blocks away from his home at PBL.

It took him three days to die of his injuries, but I have heard tell that the first thing he said when the paramedics reached him was that it was not the train conductor's fault.

* * *

Ricketts' death loosely coincided with the decline of the sardine industry—a decline he predicted—and the building stood vacant for a number of years as the once-bustling industrial neighborhood withered around it. It was rented in 1951 by Harlan Watkins, an English teacher at Monterey High School who lived there and would teach Steinbeck's *Cannery Row* to his students by having them come to the place that inspired it and read it aloud. In 1958, Watkins moved to Europe, but not before convincing a group of men friends from the community to collectively buy PBL to use as a meeting house. Thus began the Pacific Biological Laboratory's next incarnation.

The PBL Club, as they called themselves, was not a formal men's club per se, just a group of guys that used the house to meet up regularly and have drinks, listen to music, make dinner, talk about ideas and whatever else was on their minds. All told, there were about 20 members over the years, among them notable artists and writers including three famed cartoonists: Hank Ketcham [*Dennis the Menace*], Gus Arriola [*Gordo*] and Eldon Dedini [best known for his iconic comics in *Playboy*]. Many members were avid jazz fans, and one evening in the "Party Room," the idea was hatched for a jazz festival in Monterey. In October 1958, the first Monterey Jazz Festival kicked off with performances by Louis Armstrong, Dizzy Gillespie, Max Roach, and was one of Billie Holiday's last shows. The PBL became the festival afterparty spot, scene of impromptu sets in the backyard by jazz luminaries. By that point there was no chance of disturbing the neighbors. The area was so deserted there were weeds growing in the street.

Over the years, Cannery Row has been rejuvenated as a tourist destination, anchored by the Monterey Bay Aquarium and the history of the old cannery days. Through it all, PBL continued on as a men's club, and a witness to the passing of time, physical vessel of Ricketts' legacy. In 1993, the last surviving members of the original PBL club

sold the building to the city of Monterey with the understanding that it would be preserved and shared with the public for free. That promise has been kept.

* * *

It took over two years for me to actually walk through the door of PBL and stand in the rooms where all these stories unfolded. As I waited through the pandemic and the Brigadoonian hours for tours [only on the second Saturday of the month], I had built up expectations of what I would find. Ed Ricketts raised up the original single-story house and added a ground-floor laboratory and garage, so the entrance is at the top of a flight of old wooden stairs.

The walls of both main upstairs rooms are covered with a pastiche of pictures clipped out of magazines, museum prints of paintings by Botero, Goya, Matisse and others, music posters of jazz greats, and photographs of club members and of course Ricketts and Steinbeck. The front room was used for playing cards and chess and listening to music from the ample record collection. The stereo and record player are watched over by a painting of a writing John Steinbeck by local artist Judith Deim, hung right next to the front window so he has a view out to the street he immortalized.

Through a blue door covered with various coats of arms sits the Party Room. A piano on the right, a long bar along the opposite wall, the windows at the back of the house look out to the bay. Behind the bar, a series of wood cubbies are filled with various bottles of the club members' favorites tipple, each cubby labeled with the corresponding member's name, and a door leads to a tiny galley kitchen that is not much different from when Ricketts lived there, I imagine. The painting of a voluptuous female nude hanging above the piano I recognized as one of Dedini's, no doubt from seeing his work in my grandfather's old stash of *Playboy* magazines in his garage. Next to it but hidden behind the door from the front room is another of Dedini's illustrations—this one of Louis Armstrong on a poster for the first Monterey Jazz Festival.

The door off the Party Room leads to a balcony and set of wood stairs that access the backyard of the property. This is where those impromptu musical performance would take place, next to the large cement tanks once filled with "little beasties," Ricketts' affectionate name for the specimens he collected. And beyond it all, the Monterey Bay laps quietly and calmly on the rocks. In Ricketts' day, this stair access to the yard did not exist. The only way to enter was through the backdoor of the laboratory and garage on the ground floor.

Even though the original contents are now in the lobby of the Monterey Bay Aquarium just down the street, Ricketts' old lab still has a few old bottles and specimens sitting on its raw-wood shelves, and a large travel desk that was made for his specimen-gathering expeditions but proved too unwieldy for travel.

It's a ghost of the room it once was to be sure, but there is enough there to imagine how it used to be—a smelly workplace filled with slimy, fishy things being preserved in jars, and all the equipment needed to do so hanging from its walls. This was undeniably Ed Ricketts' soul space: the place where he spent the most potent, and I hope happy, part of his life. It is where he was rooted in his life's purpose. His genuine interest, appreciation and acceptance for all types of earthly creatures made this humble wood shack the unlikely epicenter for groundbreaking ideas in marine biology, literature, art, jazz history, and was a symbol for California bohemia itself.

I have spent a fair amount of time within these rooms now. I have photographed the space in depth and have been able to scan the art on the walls and the books still on the shelves from the PBL club days, and ogle the specimen jars and Ricketts' carefully typed notes on color-coded index cards in his former lab. I have yet to tire of exploring it. And at noon, that steam whistle that originally lured me here is a deafening and jarring surprise. It turns out the whistle is right next door, a siren's call not only to the past but to Pacific Biological Laboratories itself.

LESLIE WILLIAMSON is an artist, photographer and writer, and author of four books including *Still Lives: In the Homes of Artists, Great and Unsung*. Her photographs of Pacific Biological Laboratories can be seen on the Still Lives Portal of her website: *lesliewilliamson.com*.

FIVE POEMS

Written by **ROBINSON JEFFERS**

MOUNTAIN PINES

In scornful upright loneliness they stand,
Counting themselves no kin of anything
Whether of earth or sky. Their gnarled roots cling
Like wasted fingers of a clutching hand
In the grim rock. A silent spectral band
They watch the old sky, but hold no communing
With aught. Only, when some lone eagle's wing
Flaps past above their grey and desolate land,
Or when the wind pants up a rough-hewn glen,
Bending them down as with an age of thought,
Or when, 'mid flying clouds that can not dull
Her constant light, the moon shines silver, then
They find a soul, and their dim moan is wrought
Into a singing sad and beautiful.

SONG OF QUIETNESS

Drink deep, drink deep of quietness,
And on the margins of the sea
Remember not thine old distress
Nor all the miseries to be.
Calmer than mists, and cold
As they, that fold on fold
Up the dim valley are rolled,
Learn thou to be.
The Past—it was a feverish dream,
A drunken slumber full of tears.
The Future—O what wild wings gleam,
Wheeled in the van of desperate years!
Thou lovedst the evening: dawn
Glimmers; the night is gone—
What dangers lure thee on,
What dreams more fierce?
But meanwhile, now the east is gray,
The hour is pale, the cocks yet dumb,
Be glad before the birth of day,
Take thy brief rest ere morning come:
Here in the beautiful woods
All night the sea-mist floods—
Thy last of solitudes,
Thy yearlong home.

THE TREASURE

Mountains, a moment's earth-waves rising and hollowing;
 the earth too's an ephemerid; the stars—
Short-lived as grass the stars quicken in the nebula and
 dry in their summer, they spiral
Blind up space, scattered black seeds of a future; nothing
 lives long, the whole sky's
Recurrences tick the seconds of the hours of the ages of
 the gulf before birth, and the gulf
After death is like dated: to labor eighty years in a notch of
 eternity is nothing too tiresome,
Enormous repose after, enormous repose before, the flash
 of activity.
Surely you never have dreamed the incredible depths
 were prologue and epilogue merely
To the surface play in the sun, the instant of life, what is
 called life? I fancy
That silence is the thing, this noise a found word for it;
 interjection, a jump of the breath at that silence;
Stars burn, grass grows, men breathe: as a man finding
 treasure says 'Ah!' but the treasure's the essence;
Before the man spoke it was there, and after he has
 spoken he gathers it, inexhaustible treasure.

WONDER AND JOY

The things that one grows tired of—O, be sure
They are only foolish artificial things!
Can a bird ever tire of having wings?
And I, so long as life and sense endure,
[Or brief be they!] shall nevermore inure
My heart to the recurrence of the springs,
Of gray dawns, the gracious evenings,
The infinite wheeling stars. A wonder pure
Must ever well within me to behold
Venus decline; or great Orion, whose belt
Is studded with three nails of burning gold,
Ascend the winter heaven. Who never felt
This wondering joy may yet be good or great:
But envy him not: he is not fortunate.

FIRST GRASS

It rained three autumn days; then close to frost
Under clear starlight the night shivering was.
The dawn rose cold and colorless as glass,
And when we wakened rains and clouds were lost.
The ocean surged and shouted stormy-tossed.
I went down to companion him. Alas,
What faint voice by the way? The sudden grass
Cried with thin lips as I the valley crossed,
Saying blade by blade, "Although the warm sweet rain
Awakened us, this world is all too cold.
We never dreamed it thus."—"Your champion bold
Is risen," I said; "he in an hour or twain
Will comfort you." I passed. Above the dune
Stood the wan splendorless daylight-waning moon.

ROBINSON JEFFERS [1887-1962] made his long-time home at Tor House in Carmel. In his poetry, he delved deeply into the natural world of the California coast, putting wild beauty at the center of his work. Deeply influential in American poetry, Jeffers remains a central figure in the region's literary heritage.

DIRECTORY & INDEX

DIRECTORY

Notable points on [and just off] Highway 1, north to south.

Old Coast Road *route*
Natural Bridges State Marine Reserve *natural site*
Wilder Ranch State Park *natural site*
Seymour Marine Discovery Center *science center*
Arroyo Seco Canyon Trail *natural site*
Mission Santa Cruz *culture center*
La Selva Beach *natural site*
Elkhorn Yacht Club *recreation*
Monterey Bay Aquarium Research Institute *science center*
Big Sur Artworks *shop*
Salinas River *natural site*
17-Mile Drive *route*
Pebble Beach Golf Links *recreation*
Carmel Mission *culture center*
Burst + Bloom *shop*
River House Books *shop*
Monastery Beach *natural site*
Point Lobos State Natural Reserve *natural site*
Tickle Pink Inn *lodging*
Monterey Bay National Marine Sanctuary *natural site*
China Lookout *natural site*
Garrapata State Park *natural site*
Granite Creek Bouldering Area *natural site*
Rocky Creek Bridge *landmark*
Bixby Creek Bridge *landmark*
Brazil Ranch *natural site*
Mill Creek *natural site*
Hurricane Point *natural site*
Great Sur Turnout *natural site*
Little Sur River *natural site*
Point Sur State Historic Park *culture center*
Andrew Molera State Park *natural site*
Big Sur River Inn *lodging*
Big Sur Village General Store *shop*
Manuel Peak *natural site*
Ripplewood Resort *lodging*
Glen Oaks Big Sur *lodging*
Big Sur Grange *culture center*
Fernwood Camground and Resort *lodging*
Big Sur Lodge *lodging*
Pfeiffer Big Sur State Park *natural site*
Big Sur Taphouse *restaurant*
Mother Botanical & Shop *shop*
Big Sur Bakery *restaurant*
Ventana Campground *lodging*
Post Ranch Inn *lodging*
Sierra Mar *restaurant*
Alila Ventana *lodging*
The Sur House *restaurant*
Nepenthe *restaurant*
Phoenix Shop *shop*
Hawthorne Gallery *culture center*
Henry Miller Memorial Library *culture center*
Deetjen's Big Sur Inn *lodging*
Seal Beach Overlook *natural site*
COAST Big Sur *shop*
Tanbark Trail *natural site*
Partington Cove *natural site*
Julia Pfeiffer Burns State Park *natural site*
Esalen Institute *culture center*
Lucia Lodge *lodging*
New Camaldoli Hermitage *culture center*
Limekiln State Park *natural site*
Sand Dollar Beach *natural site*
Treebones Resort *lodging*
Whale Watchers Cafe *restaurant*
Big Sur Lookout *natural area*
Nathaniel Owings Memorial Redwood Grove *natural site*
Salmon Creek Trailhead *natural site*
Point Sierra Nevada *natural site*
Piedras Blancas *natural site*
Hearst Castle *landmark*
Hearst Ranch Winery *restaurant*
Cambria Beach Lodge *lodging*
Fiscalini Ranch Preserve *natural site*
Morro Strand State Beach *natural site*

INDEX

17-Mile Drive 13, 34
Alexander, Jeannie 21
Alfredo's Cantina 19
Alila Ventana 18, 20
Alta 18, 28
Andrew Molera State Park 13, 59
Apéro Club 19
Asilomar 20
Aubergine 18
Baez, Joan 52, 62
Barker, Eric 40
Barry, Jim 76
Bass, Ellen 40, 52
Bayonet 25
Between Pacific Tides 68, 108
Big Share, The 11
Big Sur [novel] 14, 40, 49, 53
Big Sur Bakery 18, 30, 94
Big Sur Folk Festival 62
Big Sur Guides 24
Big Sur International Marathon 10, 25
Big Sur Podcast, A 10
Big Sur River Inn 19
Big Sur Roundup 10
Big Sur Taphouse 18, 30
Big Sur Village 30
Big Sur Village General Store 22
Bioluminesence 67, 73
Bixby Creek Bridge 10, 15, 69
Bookshop Santa Cruz 30
Brautigan, Richard 40
Brooke-Kothlow, George 57
Bubel, MacKenzie 75
Burnett, Joe 21
Burnett, Nancy 71
Burns Creek House 57
Burst + Bloom 22
Cambria 31, 33
Cambria Beach Lodge 31
Camping 15, 101
Cannery Row [novel] 14, 44, 68, 107
Cannery Row [street] 28, 71, 107
Carmel 27, 47, 56
Carmel Art Association 23
Carmel Pine Cone 58
Carmel River State Beach 27
Carmel Valley Ranch 25
Castroville 31
Celebration at Big Sur, The 14, 62
Center for Photographic Art 12
Chase, Joseph Smeaton 43
Cheese Shop, The 22, 27
Chez Noir 19
COAST 22, 33
Coastlands House 57
Cooper Molera Adobe 28
Crews, Judson 40
Crops 63
D.L. James House 57
Dark watchers 100
Davis, Laura 40, 52
Deep-sea creatures 72
Deetjen's 18, 20, 30, 104
Duarte's Tavern 19
EagleRider 10
Earthbound Farm 19
East of Eden 7, 44
East Village, Cambria 31
Eastwood, Clint 19, 47
Ecosystems 67
El Charrito 19, 29
Elkhorn Slough Reserve 12, 70
Elkhorn Yacht Club 25
Elroy's Fine Foods 19
Erosion 15
Esalen Institute 37, 51, 52, 62, 93
Esselen Tribe 21, 41
Fall House 57, 85
Ferlinghetti, Lawrence 40, 53
Fernwood Resort 20, 30

Fin + Forage 90
Fishwife 28
Flying Fish Grill 27
Fort Ord National Monument 24
Fougeron, Anne 57, 85
French, Nora May 61
Gafill, Kirk 88
Garrapata State Park 13
Giant Artichoke 31
Ginsberg, Allen 49, 51
Glass House, The 57
Glen Oaks Big Sur 20
Granite Creek 24
Griggs, Gary 84
Grof, Stanislav 52
Hamilton, Sam 7
Harlan, Bree 96
Hawthorne Gallery 10
Hearst Castle 33, 57
Heisig, Kurt 23
Henry Miller Memorial Library 11, 22, 40, 55, 80
Hermits of Big Sur 14
Hopkins Marine Station 12
Hopkins, Nancy 40
Hotel Carmel 20
Humble Sea 19
Huxley, Aldous 51, 52
Huxley, Laura 52
Iselin, Josie 76
Jeffers, Robinson 40, 57, 60, 100, 113
Jenkins, Jedidiah 100
Keeling Curve 59
Keener, Eric 90
Kelp forests 35, 67, 68
Kerouac, Jack 14, 40, 49, 51, 53
Ketcham, Hank 25, 109
Klinger, Lee 21
KSQD 10
La Balena 19
La Bicyclette 19
La Playa Carmel 20
Land of Calm Abiding 59
Leonard, George 52
Limekiln State Park 13
Lindborg, Lance 23
Little Sur River 12
Lowpass 23
Lucia Lodge 20, 36
Lucy's On Lighthouse 28
Manganese 11
Maslow, Abraham 52
McKinnon, Laura 93
Mill Creek 24
Miller, Henry 40, 55
Miranda, Deborah A. 14, 40
Mission San Antonio de Padua 12
Mission Trail Nature Preserve 25
Mitteldorf Preserve 24
Molly, Emmaline 23
Monastery Beach 13
Monroe, Marilyn 60
Monte, Johnathan 23
Monterey 28
Monterey Bay Aquarium 12, 28, 35, 71, 75, 76, 109
Monterey Bay Aquarium Research Institute 12, 71, 74, 75, 76
Monterey Bay Equestrian Center 25
Monterey Bay National Marine Sanctuary 12, 66
Monterey Glassworks 23
Monterey International Pop Festival 46
Monterey Jazz Festival 10, 28, 109
Monterey Museum of Art 12
Morro Bay 31
Morro Strand State Beach 31
Mother Botanical 22
Mount Manuel 24
Muennig, Mickey 10, 20, 54, 57
Mulligan, Catherine 94
Murphy, Michael 51
Nason, Tom Little Bear 21
Nathaniel Owings Redwood Grove 33
National Steinbeck Center 29
Natural Bridges State Marine Reserve 12, 30
Nepenthe 11,18, 30, 88

Nephrite jade 11
New Camaldoli Hermitage 36, 59
O'Neil, Carol 83
O'Sullivan, John 76
Old Capitol Books 22
Old Coast Road 13
Pacific Biological Laboratories 107
Pacific Grove Golf Links 25
Pacific Grove Monarch Butterfly Sanctuary 28, 70
Packard, David 71
Packard, Julie 71
Palafox, Martín 87
Partington Cove 24, 30
Paso Robles 31
Passionfish 19
Pebble Beach Golf Links 34, 54
Perls, Fritz 52
Pezzini Farms 21
Pfeiffer Beach 11, 35
Phoenix Shop 22, 30
Piedras Blancas 12, 70
Pilgrim's Way 22
Pleasure of Writing 22
Point Lobos State Natural Reserve 13, 70
Point Sierra Nevada 25
Point Sur Lighthouse 83
Post Ranch Inn 18, 20, 54, 87
Prewitt Ridge 25
Price, Lilli-Anne 23
Price, Richard 51
Redwood forest 11
Research vessels 74
Reznor, Trent 58
Ricketts, Ed 68, 74, 107
Ripplewood Resort 20
Rolf, Ida 52
Roosevelt, Eleanor 47
Ross, Lillian Bos 14, 40, 47
Salinan block 11
Salinas 29
Salinas Aquatic Center 25
Salinas River 25
Salinas Valley 29
Sam Trotter House 57
Sand Dollar Beach 24, 36
Santa Cruz 30
Sardines 50
Scenic drives 13
Schicketanz, Mary Ann 23, 61
Sea Otter Classic 25
Seamount 11
Seefeldt, David 23
Seventh & Dolores 27
Ship *Los Angeles* 42
Shop, The 22
Sierra Mar 18
Slate's Hot Springs 43
Sontag, Susan 52
South Coast 36, 82, 96
South Coast Ridge Road 13
Southern sea otters 69
Spiegelberg, Frederic 51, 52
Stationæry 19
Steakley, Douglas 21
Steinbeck, John 7, 14, 40, 44, 74, 100, 107
Steller, Diana 21
Steller's jay 41
Stevenson, Robert Louis 48
Sullivan, Mark 23
Summerhill, Daniel B. 23
Sur House, The 18
Sykes Hot Springs 24
Tanbark Trail 24
Tassajara Zen Mountain Center 59
Thompson, Hunter S. 53
Tide pools 11, 71
Tor House 57, 60
Torén, Magnus 10, 80
Treebones 18, 20
Tuitele-Lewis, Jeannette 21
Venus Spirits 19
Warrick, Jonathan 21
Watkins, Harlan 109
Watts, Alan 37, 51, 52
Watts, Anne 52
Western Flyer 74
Weston Beach 12
Williamson, Leslie 107
Winter, Ella 40
Wong, Victor 53
Zantman Art Galleries 27